Table of Contents W9-CGP-931

Introduction

What Is Readers' Theater?

One good way to gain an understanding of readers' theater is to first get a clear picture of what it is *not*. Readers' theater is not a fully-staged production with sets, costumes, and dramatic action performed by actors who memorize lines from a script. Instead, a readers' theater performance is a dramatic reading, just as its name suggests. Readers are usually seated, reading from a script that is held in their hands or placed on a music stand in front of them. There may be minimal use of costumes or props, such as hats, a scepter or crown, or a simple backdrop to provide a suggestion of the setting and characters that the readers hope to bring to life for the audience during their dramatic reading.

Readers' theater offers all the enrichment of traditional theater productions, but without the logistical challenges that come with designing and building sets and creating costumes. Students are spared the stress of having to memorize lines, and can instead focus on developing a strong dramatic reading of the script.

How to Integrate *Readers' Theater* into Your Classroom

The *Readers' Theater* scripts may be used in a variety of settings for a range of educational purposes. Consider the following:

Language Arts blocks are ideal for incorporating *Readers' Theater* scripts, with their emphasis on reading aloud with expression. Many of the follow-up activities that accompany each script address key skills from the reading/language arts curriculum.

Content-Area Instruction can come alive when you use a *Readers' Theater* script to help explore social studies, science, or math concepts. Check the Table of Contents for the grade-level content-area connections in each script.

Integrated Thematic Teaching can continue throughout the day when you use *Readers' Theater* scripts to help you maintain your thematic focus across all areas of the curriculum, from language arts instruction through content-area lessons.

School Assemblies and Holiday Programs provide the perfect opportunity to showcase student performances. Consider presenting a *Readers' Theater* performance for Black History Month, Women's History Month, for parent evenings, or any other occasion when your students are invited to perform.

Teaching the *Readers' Theater* Units

The 15 units in this volume each include the following:

- A **teacher page** to help you plan instruction:

A short **summary** gives you an overview of each script's plot.

Use the **number of parts** to choose the number of readers to assign per role. Or, you may wish to create two or more casts for each production.

Background information provides facts that you may need to know about the subject treated in the script. It also guides you in activating students' prior knowledge or in building background about new or unfamiliar topics. This helps promote success for students as they approach each new script.

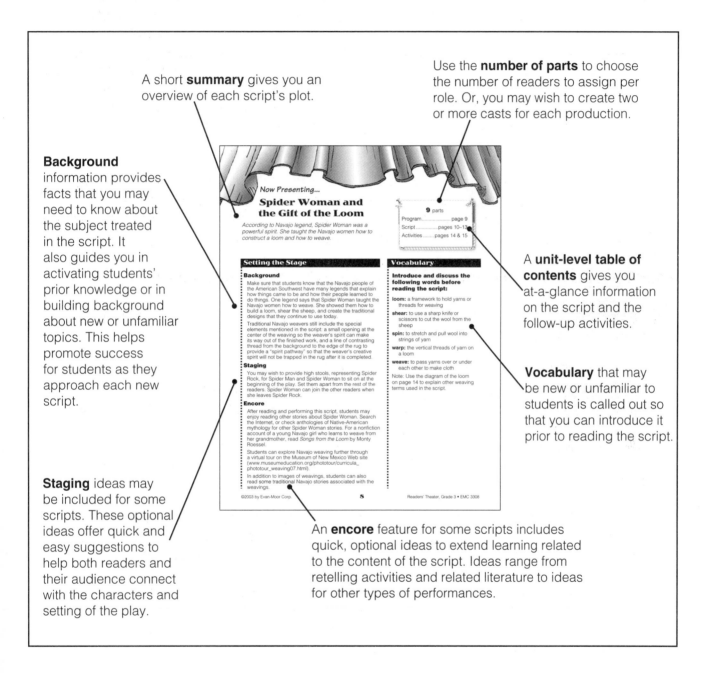

Now Presenting...

Spider Woman and the Gift of the Loom

According to Navajo legend, Spider Woman was a powerful spirit. She taught the Navajo women how to construct a loom and how to weave.

9 parts
Program .... page 9
Script .... pages 10–13
Activities .... pages 14 & 15

Setting the Stage

Background

Make sure that students know that the Navajo people of the American Southwest have many legends that explain how things came to be and how their people learned to do things. One legend says that Spider Woman taught the Navajo women how to weave. She showed them how to build a loom, shear the sheep, and create the traditional designs that they continue to use today.

Traditional Navajo weavers still include the special elements mentioned in the script: a small opening at the center of the weaving so the weaver's spirit can make its way out of the finished work, and a line of contrasting thread from the background to the edge of the rug to provide a "spirit pathway" so that the weaver's creative spirit will not be trapped in the rug after it is completed.

Staging

You may wish to provide high stools, representing Spider Rock, for Spider Man and Spider Woman to sit on at the beginning of the play. Set them apart from the rest of the readers. Spider Woman can join the other readers when she leaves Spider Rock.

Encore

After reading and performing this script, students may enjoy reading other stories about Spider Woman. Search the Internet, or check anthologies of Native-American mythology for other Spider Woman stories. For a nonfiction account of a young Navajo girl who learns to weave from her grandmother, read *Songs from the Loom* by Monty Roessel.

Students can explore Navajo weaving further through a virtual tour on the Museum of New Mexico Web site (www.museumeducation.org/phototour/curricula_ phototour_weaving07.html).

In addition to images of weavings, students can also read some traditional Navajo stories associated with the weavings.

©2003 by Evan-Moor Corp.   **8**   Readers' Theater, Grade 3 • EMC 3308

Vocabulary

Introduce and discuss the following words before reading the script:

loom: a framework to hold yarns or threads for weaving

shear: to use a sharp knife or scissors to cut the wool from the sheep

spin: to stretch and pull wool into strings of yarn

warp: the vertical threads of yarn on a loom

weave: to pass yarns over or under each other to make cloth

Note: Use the diagram of the loom on page 14 to explain other weaving terms used in the script.

A **unit-level table of contents** gives you at-a-glance information on the script and the follow-up activities.

Vocabulary that may be new or unfamiliar to students is called out so that you can introduce it prior to reading the script.

Staging ideas may be included for some scripts. These optional ideas offer quick and easy suggestions to help both readers and their audience connect with the characters and setting of the play.

An **encore** feature for some scripts includes quick, optional ideas to extend learning related to the content of the script. Ideas range from retelling activities and related literature to ideas for other types of performances.

- A reproducible **program** page provides an introduction to the script and a list of characters. Use this page to list the names of students who will read each role, and distribute it to your audience to enhance the theater-going experience.

- The **script** is the heart of the *Readers' Theater* volume. This is the reproducible four- or five-page text that students will read during rehearsals and performances. You may wish to read the script aloud to students before assigning parts and beginning rehearsal readings. Once you have read through the script as a group, you may wish to assign students to work independently in small groups while you interact with other student groups.

- Two or three pages of follow-up **activities** may be assigned once students have completed a first reading of the script. Activities are designed to be completed independently, and may be conducted while you provide individualized or small-group instruction or hold a rehearsal with another group of students.

Meeting Individual Needs

Struggling readers may be partnered with one or more stronger readers who all read the same role together. This group support is often enough to allow struggling readers to participate fully in the activity. Struggling readers may also be able to independently read parts that have a repeating refrain or a simple rhyme pattern.

Students acquiring English may benefit from using the same approaches as for struggling readers. In addition, you may wish to create an audio recording of the script to provide English learners the opportunity to listen to fluent English pronunciation of the script as they follow along with the written text.

Accelerated learners may be challenged to transform *Readers' Theater* scripts into fully-staged productions by adding stage directions, planning props and sets, and even developing or expanding the existing dialog. You might also use such students as "directors," helping to manage small-group rehearsals for class *Readers' Theater* productions.

Evaluating Student Performance

Use the templates provided on pages 5 and 6 to help students plan and evaluate their performances. You may copy and distribute the templates just as they are, or use them to guide you in leading a class discussion about the criteria for evaluating *Readers' Theater* performances. Students may also develop their own iconography (e.g., one or two thumbs up, thumbs down, 1 to 5 stars, etc.) to rate their own performances and those of their classmates. Encourage students to be thoughtful in providing feedback, stressing the importance of sharing ways to improve, as well as highlighting successful aspects of the performance. You may wish to conduct performance reviews during the rehearsal stage in order to give students an opportunity to incorporate suggestions for improvement. You may also wish to compare those comments to feedback following the final performance. Use the template on page 7 to conduct your own assessment of students' acquisition of language arts skills during *Readers' Theater* activities.

Pre-performance Checklist

Name _____

1. Did you listen to a reading of the script?
   ☐ **Yes**
   ☐ **No** – Ask your teacher, another adult, or a classmate to read it to you.

2. Did you highlight all your lines in the script?
   ☐ **Yes**
   ☐ **No** – Use a highlighting pen to go over all your lines.

3. Did you mark places where you must pause between lines?
   ☐ **Yes**
   ☐ **No** – Use a mark like this: / /

4. Have you collected any materials or props that you will use?
   ☐ **Yes**
   ☐ **No** – Ask your teacher or other cast members for ideas if you need help.

5. Have you chosen and practiced any movements, faces, or speaking styles you will use?
   ☐ **Yes**
   ☐ **No** – Ask your teacher or other cast members for ideas if you need help.

6. Have you practiced reading your lines with expression?
   ☐ **Yes**
   ☐ **No** – Try out your ideas with a partner or another cast member.

7. Have you participated in a rehearsal and gotten performance feedback?
   ☐ **Yes**
   ☐ **No** – Have a reviewer focus on your participation in the play. After you get feedback, find ways to make changes to improve your performance.

Performance Review Template

Date: _____ Title of play: _____

☐ Rehearsal
☐ Performance

1. I am reviewing
   ☐ one reader   Name: _____   Role: _____
   ☐ the entire performance

2. I could see the reader(s).
   ☐ Yes
   ☐ Needs improvement   Name(s): _____

3. I could hear the reader(s).
   ☐ Yes
   ☐ Needs to speak more loudly   Name(s): _____

4. I could understand the reader(s).
   ☐ Yes
   ☐ Needs to speak more clearly   Name(s): _____

5. The reader(s) used good expression.
   ☐ Yes
   ☐ Needs to improve   Name(s): _____

6. The use of gestures was
   ☐ just right
   ☐ not enough; use more
   ☐ too much; use fewer   Name(s): _____

Other comments:

_____

_____

_____

_____

Assessing Oral Presentations

As you observe students during rehearsals or performances, focus on the following areas in assessing individual students.

Date: _____

Title of play: _____

☐ Rehearsal

☐ Performance

Name: _____ Role: _____

1. Student speaks clearly. ☐ Yes ☐ Needs improvement

2. Student speaks at appropriate pace. ☐ Yes ☐ Needs improvement

3. Student speaks fluently, using appropriate intonation, expression, and emphasis. ☐ Yes ☐ Needs improvement

4. Student enlivens reading with gestures and facial expressions. ☐ Yes ☐ Needs improvement

5. Student prepared and used appropriate props. ☐ Yes ☐ Not applicable

6. Student participated actively in rehearsals. ☐ Yes ☐ Needs improvement

7. Student contributed appropriately to this production. ☐ Yes ☐ Needs improvement

Other comments: _____

_____

_____

_____

_____

Now Presenting...

Spider Woman and the Gift of the Loom

According to Navajo legend, Spider Woman was a powerful spirit. She taught the Navajo women how to construct a loom and how to weave.

Setting the Stage

Background

Make sure that students know that the Navajo people of the American Southwest have many legends that explain how things came to be and how their people learned to do things. One legend says that Spider Woman taught the Navajo women how to weave. She showed them how to build a loom, shear the sheep, and create the traditional designs that they continue to use today.

Traditional Navajo weavers still include the special elements mentioned in the script: a small opening at the center of the weaving so that the weaver's spirit can make its way out of the finished work, and a line of contrasting thread from the background to the edge of the rug to provide a "spirit pathway" so that the weaver's creative spirit will not be trapped in the rug after it is completed.

Staging

You may wish to provide high stools, representing Spider Rock, for Spider Man and Spider Woman to sit on at the beginning of the play. Set them apart from the rest of the readers. Spider Woman can join the other readers when she leaves Spider Rock.

Encore

After reading and performing this script, students may enjoy reading other stories about Spider Woman. Search the Internet, or check anthologies of Native American mythology for other Spider Woman stories. For a nonfiction account of a young Navajo girl who learns to weave from her grandmother, read *Songs from the Loom* by Monty Roessel.

Students can explore Navajo weaving further through a virtual tour on the Museum of New Mexico Web site (www.museumeducation.org/phototour/curricula_ phototour_weaving07.html).

In addition to images of weavings, students can also read some traditional Navajo stories associated with the weavings.

Vocabulary

Introduce and discuss the following words before reading the script:

loom: a framework to hold yarns or threads for weaving

shear: to use a sharp knife or scissors to cut the wool from the sheep

spin: to stretch and pull wool into strings of yarn

warp: the vertical threads of yarn on a loom

weave: to pass yarns over or under each other to make cloth

Note: Use the diagram of the loom on page 14 to explain other weaving terms used in the script.

Spider Woman and the Gift of the Loom

Spider Woman gives a great gift to the Navajo people.

Characters

Spider Woman .... _____

Spider Man............................. _____

Navajo Woman 1 .... _____

Navajo Woman 2 .... _____

Navajo Woman 3 .... _____

Navajo Man............................. _____

Narrator 1 .... _____

Narrator 2 .... _____

Chorus .... _____

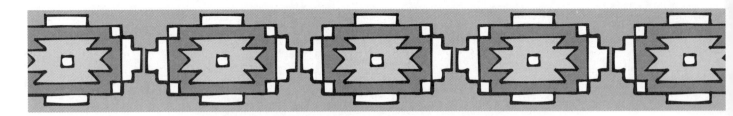

Spider Woman and the Gift of the Loom

.... **Characters** ....

Spider Woman
Spider Man
Navajo Woman 1
Navajo Woman 2
Navajo Woman 3

Navajo Man
Narrator 1
Narrator 2
Chorus

Narrator 1: Long, long ago, the Navajo people were very hungry. Their clothes were thin. Sometimes they were cold. Other times the sun beat down and made them too hot. They did not know how to help themselves. It was a sad, scary time for the People.

Narrator 2: Spider Man and Spider Woman lived high above the Navajo people at the top of Spider Rock. As they looked down at the suffering People, their hearts were moved.

Spider Man: We must help the People. I will make a loom. You can take it to them and show them how to weave.

Narrator 1: Spider Woman took the loom. She left Spider Rock and went down among the People. She assembled the loom where all could see it.

Navajo Man: What is this?

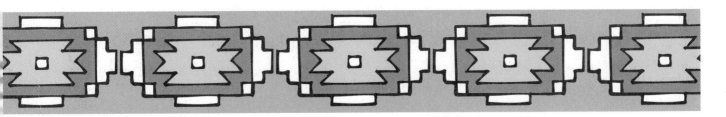

Spider Woman: It is a loom. My husband, Spider Man, built it for you. The top of the loom is like the sky. The bottom is like the earth. The strings that hold the loom and frame together are like the lightning. The warp is like the falling rain.

Navajo Man: What does it do? How will it help us?

Spider Woman: Be patient and you will see. Since the women tend the sheep, they should be the ones to learn what to do. Let the women come with me now.

Narrator 2: Spider Woman took all the women to the place where the sheep were grazing.

Narrator 1: She showed them how to use a sharp knife to shear the sheep.

Narrator 2: Next, she showed them how to wash the wool.

Narrator 1: After that, Spider Woman showed the women how to straighten the wool and spin it into yarn.

Woman 1: The black and white yarns are so pretty. We can mix them together to make gray.

Woman 2: I think we should have more colors. We can use plants and berries to dye the wool.

Woman 3: *(looking at the loom)* There must be a way to attach the yarn to this loom. Is that right, Spider Woman?

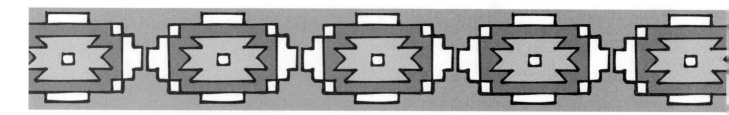

Spider Woman: Yes, let me show you. Then I will teach you how to make blankets and rugs.

Narrator 2: Soon the loom was ready. Spider Woman wove a beautiful pattern. She removed the finished rug from the loom.

Woman 1: This is lovely! Now I understand. If we weave rugs and blankets, they will protect us from the heat and cold. And we will take joy in looking at their beauty.

Woman 2: How will we know what patterns to use? Spider Woman, will you draw the design you used for us?

Spider Woman: No, you do not need drawings. Think beautiful thoughts about the land and the sky. Form pictures of the mountains and the clouds and the other things of nature in your mind. Listen to your minds and hearts. They will tell you what your patterns should be.

Woman 3: I think we should leave a small opening in the middle so that our minds and spirits can get through.

Woman 1: Yes, and we should weave a pathway, too, to guide them. It can be a different colored yarn. It should go from the center to the edge.

Spider Woman: These are good ideas. You have learned well. I will leave you now.

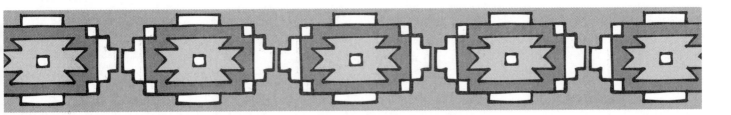

Narrator 1: The women worked and worked. Soon they had many finished blankets and rugs.

Navajo Man: These rugs and blankets are wonderful. I will take some of them to other places and trade them for food and other things we need. We will never be without supplies again. We should sing a song of thanks to Spider Man and Spider Woman.

Chorus: We are weavers of beautiful rugs.
We care for the sheep
who give us wool.
We dye it the colors of the earth.
We weave our thoughts and our hearts
into our patterns.

Narrator 2: Spider Woman and Spider Man watched and listened from Spider Rock.

Spider Man: This is good. Now the People can take care of themselves.

Spider Woman: Yes, and they have a skill to pass down to their children, to their children's children, and on forever. We have done well, my husband. We need not worry any more.

Name _____

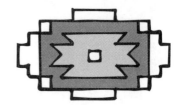

Design a Rug

Spider Woman taught the Navajo women to weave. Then they designed and wove beautiful rugs. Now you can design your own rug. Draw a pattern on this loom and then color it.

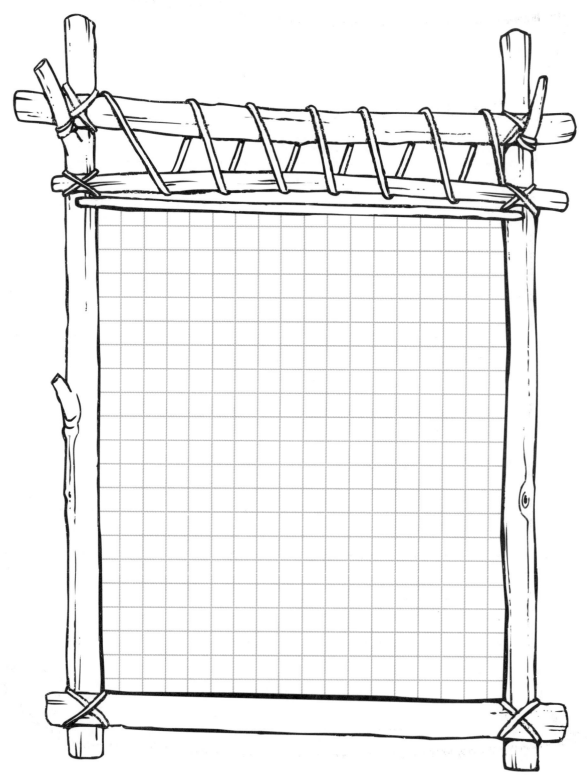

Name _____

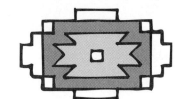

Letter to Spider Woman

Imagine that you are a Navajo weaver. Write a letter to Spider Woman. Tell her how learning to weave has changed your life.

_____
Date

Dear Spider Woman,

_____

_____

_____

_____

_____

_____

_____

_____

_____

Sincerely,

_____

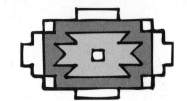

How to Weave a Rug

Order the steps for weaving a rug from 1 to 9.

_____ Straighten the wool.

_____ Wash the wool.

_____ Spin the wool.

_____ Weave the rug.

_____ Dye the wool.

_____ Raise the sheep.

_____ Set up the loom.

_____ Remove the rug from the loom.

_____ Shear the sheep.

 Readers' Theater, Grade 3 • EMC 3308

Now Presenting...

A Wild Day

A family on vacation visits the J. N. "Ding" Darling Wildlife Refuge on Sanibel Island, Florida. This 6,400-acre refuge is home to birds, amphibians, reptiles, mammals, and a mangrove forest.

Setting the Stage

Background

The National Wildlife Refuge System was established in 1903 by President Theodore Roosevelt. It now includes 93 million acres of land and waterways in the United States, providing protected habitats for fish, birds, other wildlife, and plants. Visitors to these refuges may observe and photograph nature. In some refuges, hunting and fishing are also permitted. Many of the refuges have educational programs led by naturalists, as in this script set in the J. N. "Ding" Darling Wildlife Refuge on Sanibel Island in Florida.

Staging

The person reading the part of the guide may wear a badge that says "Wildlife Refuge Guide." You might invite those reading the family's parts to wear sun visors or sunglasses.

Encore

Encourage students to learn more about the National Wildlife Refuge System by visiting these Web sites:

- National Wildlife Refuge Association (www.refugenet.org/nwr-overview.htm)
- The J. N. "Ding" Darling National Wildlife Refuge (www.dingdarlingsociety.org)
- U.S. Fish and Wildlife Service, National Wildlife Refuges (http://ifw2irm2.irm1.r2.fws.gov/refuges)

You might also enjoy sharing a book about wildlife refuges (available in English and Spanish) called *Wildlife Refuge: A Classroom Adventure* by Lorraine Ward.

Vocabulary

Introduce and discuss the following words before reading the script. Then ask students to identify the words that name animals.

amphibian: an animal that can live on land and in the water

kayak: a type of canoe designed to be paddled by one or two people

mammal: a warmblooded animal, usually covered with hair or fur; females bear live young and produce milk

manatee: a mammal that lives in tropical waters

migrate: to move from one place to another with the change of seasons

protect: to shield or defend from injury or danger

refuge: a safe place

reptile: a coldblooded animal covered with scales

system: a set of related or connected things that form a whole

Now Presenting...

A Wild Day

Come along with the López family as they tour a wildlife refuge in Florida.

Characters

Ranger .... _____

Guide .... _____

Mr. López .... _____

Mrs. López .... _____

José .... _____

Ana... _____

A Wild Day

Ranger	Mrs. López
Guide	José
Mr. López	Ana

(at the visitor's center of the J. N. "Ding" Darling Wildlife Refuge)

Ranger: Welcome to the J. N. "Ding" Darling Wildlife Refuge. Are you here for the tour?

Mr. López: We sure are! I'm Simón López, and this is my family. I hope we're here in time for the early tour.

Ranger: You're right on time. If you'll come with me, I'll take you to meet your guide. . . Oh, here she is! Tracy, this is the López family. And this is Tracy. She'll be your guide on your visit to the refuge today.

Guide: Welcome! You're Mr. López?

Mr. López: Yes, and this is my wife, Lilia López, and our children, Ana and José.

Guide: Great to meet all of you. I'll be with you during your visit to the park.

José: Are we going to go to the rides first?

Ranger: The rides?

Ana: You know, like the Wild 'Gator, the Swallowtail, and all the other fun, scary rides.

Ranger: Tracy, I'm going to let you straighten this out. I've got to get back to the office.

Guide: Go right ahead. I'll take it from here . . . Well, José, I'm not sure what kind of an adventure you thought you were going to have today! This is definitely a park, and we do have 'gators and swallowtails here. But they're not amusement park rides! They're just two of the endangered animals that live here in this wildlife refuge.

Ana: Wildlife refuge? We thought we were visiting a wild animal park—you know, with rides and everything.

José: I thought this was going to be a really wild day.

Guide: Oh, I think it will be. We might even take a ride—but not the kind you were imagining. Come on. Let's get started. We'll do some walking first.

(out on the trail)

Mrs. López: It is so beautiful out here! When did this land become a wildlife refuge?

Guide: Actually, the first wildlife refuge was established by President Theodore Roosevelt over 100 years ago. The government has been adding others ever since then. This one became part of the system in 1978. Today there are over 530 refuges in America. That's the largest wildlife refuge system in the world.

Ana: Why are there so many refuges?

Guide: Our country needs places that are safe for wildlife to live and grow. The refuges protect the natural habitats of birds, animals, and plants. There is at least one refuge in each of our 50 states.

Mr. López: Look, kids—I see an alligator at the edge of the water!

José: Awesome!

Guide: I told you we had wild 'gators here, José. In fact, there are about 50 kinds of reptiles and amphibians here, including alligators and crocodiles. We have over 290 types of birds. And there are 32 different mammals, including raccoons and bobcats. You might even see a manatee in the water. You can look at all of them, but please don't disturb them.

Mrs. López: Do the birds live here all year?

Guide: Some of them do. Others migrate here for the winter. Since we're on the west coast of Florida, this is a warm place for them to spend the winter.

Ana: *(pointing to a group of trees)* Those trees look like they have legs coming down from the branches. And they're growing out of the water!

Guide: Those are mangrove trees. Would you like to take a kayak ride through the mangrove forest and see them up close?

José: You bet!

Ana: I am totally up for that!

Mrs. and Mr. López: That sounds great!

Guide: Then let's go back to the visitor's center and check out a few kayaks. You're in for a real treat!

(later, in the kayaks, paddling through the mangrove forest)

Ana: Why do the roots look so weird?

Guide: Mangroves grow in or near shallow water that is partly salty and partly fresh. Some of the roots get covered with water. So the mangrove has developed a special kind of root to help it breathe in the muddy ground. Some roots grow upward. Others grow down from the tree limbs.

Mrs. López: *(looking up)* I like the way the tree branches make an arch above us. It's like we're in a big, leafy tunnel. It's cool and shady in here.

José: *(smiling)* This is way better than an amusement park! I want to check out some of the other wildlife refuges!

Mr. López: That's a great idea. I'll check the Internet to see if there are any near our home in Texas.

Ana: I want a job like Tracy's when I get older.

Guide: You can do that, too. Study hard, take science classes, and learn all you can about animals and plants. I bet you'd like this job as much as I do.

Ana: Maybe I can come work here.

Guide: I hope you do! Well, it's time to start paddling back to the visitor's center.

José: This day's been a lot wilder than I could have imagined. Wildlife is cool!

Ana: And so are wildlife refuges!

Name _____

Wildlife Sort

Cut out the pictures. Glue them in the correct categories.

Birds and Butterflies	Reptiles and Amphibians	Mammals

alligator   manatee   pelican

bobcat   raccoon   tree frog

heron   crocodile   swallowtail

Name _____

Wild Contractions

A **contraction** is a word that is made up of two words. One or two letters come out when the two words are joined together. An apostrophe takes the place of the missing letters. Read these contractions.

isn't—is not	**that's**—that is
can't—can not	**it's**—it is
you're—you are	**I'll**—I will
we're—we are	**I'm**—I am
they're—they are	**let's**—let us

Read each sentence. Write the contraction for the underlined words.

1. "You <u>can not</u> disturb the animals in a refuge," said Tracy. _____

2. "Look at the alligators. <u>They are</u> lying in the sun," said José. _____

3. "<u>Let us</u> go out in the kayaks," said Tracy. _____

4. "<u>That is</u> a huge tree," said Mrs. López. _____

5. Mr. López said, "<u>I will</u> find a refuge in Texas." _____

6. "<u>I am</u> going to work in a refuge some day," said Ana. _____

7. "<u>We are</u> glad we came," said Ana and José. _____

8. "<u>You are</u> a great guide," Mrs. López told Tracy. _____

9. "The refuge <u>is not</u> open for tours at night," said Tracy. _____

10. "<u>It is</u> time to leave now," said Mr. López. _____

Name _____

Design a Wildlife Refuge

What do you think a wildlife refuge should look like? Draw a picture of it. Include the animals and plants that would live there. Show how people would be able to look at the animals.

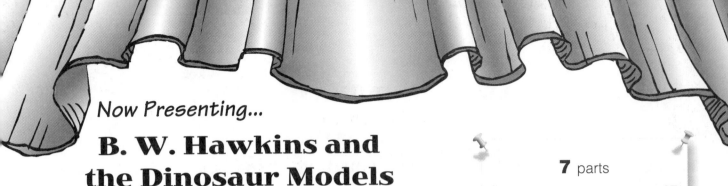

Now Presenting...

B. W. Hawkins and the Dinosaur Models

Benjamin Waterhouse Hawkins made the first dinosaur models in England in 1854. He based his models on information given to him by Richard Owen, a British scientist.

Setting the Stage

Background

Scientists found the first dinosaur bones in the early nineteenth century. A British scientist, Dr. Richard Owen, created the name *dinosaur*. Owen worked with sculptor Benjamin Waterhouse Hawkins to make the first life-sized models of these dinosaurs. They compared the fossils to the bones of modern animals, and then drew conclusions about how dinosaurs looked. Even though many of the designs Hawkins created have now been proven to be incorrect, his contributions are still valued.

Encore

After completing the activity on page 32, students may use clay to make a model of the iguanodon. Remind students that Hawkins's original drawings were incorrect. Help them use the Internet or reference books to find a contemporary rendition of an iguanodon. Discuss the similarities and differences between the two drawings.

Vocabulary

Introduce and discuss the following words before reading the script. Then ask students to predict how the words might be used in the play.

base: the part on which something else rests

fossil: the hardened remains of animal life from an earlier part of Earth's history that is preserved in Earth's crust

model: a small copy or imitation of an object

mold: a hollow form used to create a shape by filling it with a liquid that hardens

sculptor: a person who forms figures from clay, stone, metal, wood, or other materials

skeleton: a hard framework that provides support

Now Presenting...

B. W. Hawkins and the Dinosaur Models

How did people figure out what dinosaurs looked like? This is the story of a man who used his imagination—along with art and science—to develop the first ideas about how dinosaurs looked.

Characters

Narrator 1 .... _____

Narrator 2 .... _____

B. W. Hawkins .... _____

Dr. Richard Owen .... _____
(scientist)

Mr. Smythe .... _____
(assistant to B.W. Hawkins)

Meg Smythe .... _____
(8-year-old daughter)

Will Smythe .... _____
(10-year-old son)

B. W. Hawkins and the Dinosaur Models

.... **Characters** ....

Narrator 1   Mr. Smythe
Narrator 2   Meg Smythe
B. W. Hawkins   Will Smythe
Dr. Richard Owen

(Scene 1: London, England, 1854, in the workshop of B. W. Hawkins)

Narrator 1: Benjamin Waterhouse Hawkins was an unusual sculptor. He was making something that no one had ever made before. Actually, it was something that no one had ever even seen!

Narrator 2: Join us now. It is early on a Saturday morning. Hawkins is just entering his workshop. We'll watch as Hawkins and his assistants work on . . . the first dinosaur models!

Mr. Smythe: Ah, good morning, Mr. Hawkins. How are you today?

Hawkins: Fine, and ready to work. The show is only a few months away. *(smiling at Meg and Will)* Ah, I see you brought two helpers.

Meg: Oh yes, I couldn't wait to get here. We've been hearing about the tremendous creature that you and Father have been working on.

Will: We want to learn all about the dinosaurs. And we'd love to help you in any way we can.

Hawkins: Lovely! But first, allow me to present Dr. Owen. It was he who made up the word "dinosaur." He studies the fossilized bones that we have been using to build these models.

Meg and Will: Pleased to meet you, sir.

Dr. Owen: And now, meet the iguanodon.

Meg: Oh my. How fierce it looks! How on earth did you know what it looked like?

Dr. Owen: I found this tooth. It looks quite similar to the tooth of a reptile living today: the modern iguana. We believe this prehistoric creature may have been an ancestor of today's iguana. So we have used the modern iguana to help us determine the way the prehistoric iguanodon must have looked.

Will: But how did you figure out the size to make the iguanodon model?

Dr. Owen: Mr. Hawkins and I measured the fossil bones. That helped us to figure out the size of the whole beast.

Will: And then you made this big model?

Dr. Owen: Actually, I made a drawing of the beast first.

Hawkins: After that, I made a small clay model.

Mr. Smythe: Then I helped make a life-size clay model. Next, we used the clay model to make a mold for the body.

Hawkins: Then we built an iron skeleton to help add strength to the inside of our structure.

Mr. Smythe: After that we built a brick base and covered the skeleton with cement.

Hawkins: *(to Meg and Will)* That's how we ended up with this model. And now we're ready to add some color to make this creature look more lifelike. Would you two like to help paint it?

Will and Meg: Oh yes. Let's get busy!

(Scene 2: Crystal Palace Park, 1854)

Narrator 1: The models were placed in the garden of a new art and science museum near London. It was called the Crystal Palace.

Narrator 2: They were part of a grand opening celebration.

Meg: Mr. Hawkins, this is so exciting! Look at all the people here!

Hawkins: Isn't it marvelous? They say over 40,000 people have come out to celebrate the opening of the Crystal Palace.

Will: Listen to the children! They're laughing and cheering. Your dinosaur models are a big success.

Hawkins: This is a great day. My models are a window into the past. Now many people will know what the dinosaurs looked like.

Narrator 1: Let's leave our enthusiastic friends here on this grand day.

Narrator 2: Since that time, scientists have learned much more about dinosaurs. In fact, they found out that many of the models made by B. W. Hawkins were not correct.

Narrator 1: But the work of B. W. Hawkins is still important. He showed others how to build the models.

Narrator 2: And he gave people the first idea of what dinosaurs looked like. He awakened the public's interest in dinosaurs.

Narrator 1: And that led to more study and more discoveries about these prehistoric creatures.

Narrator 2: The dinosaur models created by B. W. Hawkins are still in the Crystal Palace Park. Maybe you can see them there someday.

Name _____

Build Your Own Dinosaur

B. W. Hawkins made the first dinosaur model. Now you can make one, too. Cut out the pieces on this page. Glue them together on another page to make an iguanodon like the one Hawkins made. Then draw Crystal Palace Park in the background.

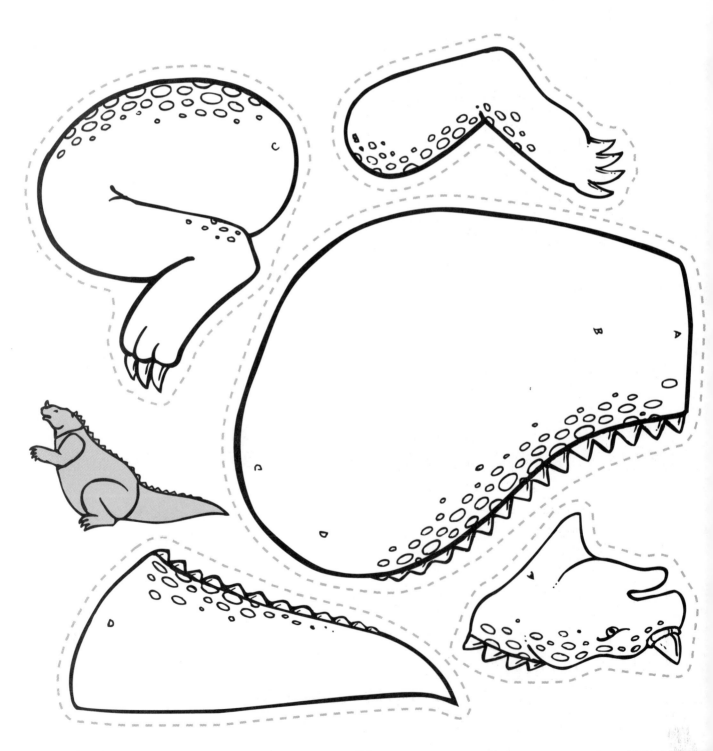

Name _____

Dear Mr. Hawkins

Imagine that you are a child who saw the dinosaurs at Crystal Palace Park in 1854. What would you like to tell B. W. Hawkins about his models? What questions would you like to ask him? Write a letter to him here.

Date:

Dear Mr. Hawkins,

Sincerely,

Put a Dinosaur Model in Order

B. W. Hawkins and his helpers did seven things to make his dinosaur models. Reread the play to find them. Then number these steps in order.

_____ They made an iron skeleton.

_____ They made a small clay model.

_____ They made a brick base.

_____ They made a life-size clay model.

_____ They made a drawing.

_____ They covered the skeleton with cement.

_____ They made a mold for the body.

Now Presenting...

The Amazing Laundry Hamper
Based on a Tale from the Brothers Grimm

In this modern adaptation of an old fairy tale, a brother and sister learn that their actions have consequences.

Setting the Stage

Background

Invite students to discuss the chores they have at home and what they do to keep their room neat and clean. Be sure to ask them what they do with their dirty clothing.

Tell students that this script is a modern adaptation of one of the European fairy tales collected by Jacob and Wilhelm Grimm in the early 1800s. The original tale was known as "Mother Holle" or "Mother Hulda." The tales that the Grimm Brothers wrote down were originally passed on orally and were designed to teach the listeners a lesson. Encourage students to speculate about what the lesson in this tale might be.

Staging

Have the person reading Chuck's part look very neat and tidy. The person reading Doris's part should look messy. The person reading the part of Mrs. Dazzle could wear costume jewelry or a fancy hat.

Encore

Read the original tale from the Brothers Grimm with students. Have them compare and contrast the two versions. Then invite individuals or partners to write their own version of the tale.

Vocabulary

Introduce and discuss the following words before reading the script:

boutique: a small shop where fashionable—and often expensive—clothing and other items are sold

display: an arrangement of items put out to be seen

hamper: a large basket, usually with a cover

laundry: a batch of clothing that has been washed, or is about to be washed

vacuum: to clean a carpeted floor using a vacuum cleaner to pick up dirt

Now Presenting...

The Amazing Laundry Hamper
Based on a Tale from the Brothers Grimm

A brother and sister's unusual adventure teaches them a valuable lesson.

Characters

Narrator 1 .... _____

Narrator 2 .... _____

Dad .... _____

Mom .... _____

Chuck (the son) .... _____

Doris (the daughter) .... _____

Mrs. Dazzle .... _____

Describe Doris and Chuck

A **character trait** tells about the way a character in a story acts or behaves. Read the list of traits in the middle of the page. Then draw a line from the trait to the character it describes.

disobedient

friendly

greedy

helpful

lazy

messy

neat

obedient

Chuck

Doris

Amazing Adjectives

An **adjective** is a word that describes, or tells more about, a naming word or noun. Write two words to describe each noun. Then draw a picture to go with the words.

a _____

_____ laundry hamper

a _____

_____ bedroom

a _____

_____ boutique

a _____

_____ morning

Name _____

What Was the Lesson?

Most fairy tales teach the reader or listener a lesson. What lesson do you think is taught in "The Amazing Laundry Hamper"? Answer these questions, and then explain the lesson from this tale.

1. How did Chuck behave?

_____

2. What reward did Chuck get?

_____

3. How did Doris behave?

_____

4. What reward did Doris get?

_____

5. What lesson do you think is told in the tale?

_____

_____

_____

_____

Now Presenting...

It Happened at Hull House

While she was still a child, Jane Addams decided she wanted to help poor people. In September 1889, she used her own money to open Hull House in a poor Chicago neighborhood. It was one of the earliest "community service centers" in America, and helped countless immigrants and poor people improve the quality of their lives.

8 parts

Setting the Stage

Background

Jane Addams was one of the foremost social activists of her time. Hull House became popular as soon as it opened. Fifty thousand people visited in the first year. Two thousand people a day stopped in during the second year. Wealthy friends and poor neighbors all volunteered at Hull House. Programs included a kindergarten, day care, art gallery, library, and classes (in English, art, music, dance, and gymnastics). Eventually the Hull House complex took up an entire city block.

Staging

Have the student reading the part of Jane Addams wear an apron. The student reading Mrs. Lobov's part could wear a scarf over her head.

Encore

To learn more about Jane Addams and her work, students can check out Ann Johnson's book, *The Value of Friendship: The Story of Jane Addams.* They can also visit the Web site for the Jane Addams Hull House Museum at the University of Illinois, Chicago (www.uic.edu/jaddams/hull/hull_house.html).

Vocabulary

To introduce and discuss unfamiliar vocabulary before reading the script, copy sentences from the play that contain these words, and then model how to use context clues to figure out their meanings.

drama: a play

immigrant: a person who comes to live in a new country

neighborhood: a community of people who live near each other

nursery: a place where parents may leave their children temporarily to be cared for by trained professionals

play: a drama or theater piece; to participate in a game or other entertainment

public: for the use of the community in general; not private

sculpture: the art of carving wood, chiseling stone, or molding clay or other material to form statues

tour: to inspect or view a particular area

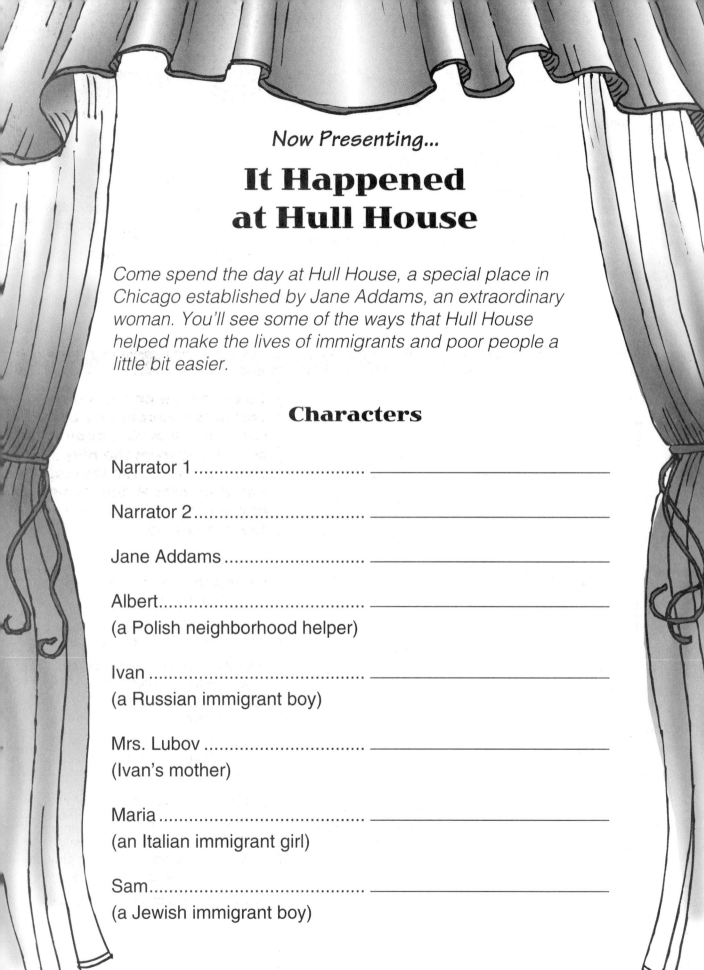

Now Presenting...

It Happened at Hull House

Come spend the day at Hull House, a special place in Chicago established by Jane Addams, an extraordinary woman. You'll see some of the ways that Hull House helped make the lives of immigrants and poor people a little bit easier.

Characters

Narrator 1 .... _____

Narrator 2 .... _____

Jane Addams .... _____

Albert....................................... _____
(a Polish neighborhood helper)

Ivan .... _____
(a Russian immigrant boy)

Mrs. Lubov .... _____
(Ivan's mother)

Maria .... _____
(an Italian immigrant girl)

Sam.. _____
(a Jewish immigrant boy)

It Happened at Hull House

········· Characters ·········

Narrator 1	Ivan
Narrator 2	Mrs. Lubov
Jane Addams	Sam
Albert	Maria

Narrator 1: Jane Addams was born in Cedarville, Illinois, in 1860. After graduating from college, she moved to Chicago, where she longed to help people in need, especially poor women and children.

Narrator 2: In 1889 she bought and moved into Hull House. This was a big, old house in a poor neighborhood in Chicago. Most of the people in the neighborhood were immigrants.

Narrator 1: Our story opens in 1905. By this time, Hull House had become a very popular place in the neighborhood.

Narrator 2: Jane Addams could speak several languages. When you read the play, imagine that you are speaking in Russian, Italian, or Yiddish—the language spoken by many Eastern European Jews. *(A knocking sound is heard.)*

Jane: *(answering the door)* Welcome. You have not been here before.

Mrs. Lubov: I am Irena Lubov. This is my son, Ivan, and my baby, Anna. We have just moved here from Russia. My neighbor, Mrs. Marco, said you would watch my children while I go to work.

Jane: Yes, I'd be glad to keep them here. There are many children who stay with us. Albert will take the baby.

Albert: *(smiling)* We have a very good nursery. Anna will have her own crib. We will play with her and feed her.

Jane: *(calling to a boy and a girl)* Maria, Sam, come here, please. This is Ivan. You two will be his special friends today and show him around.

Maria: Welcome, Ivan. I think you will like Hull House.

Sam: We all like it here. There are many fun things to do.

Narrator 1: Mrs. Lubov leaves. Maria and Sam take Ivan for a tour of Hull House.

Maria: This is the library. We can read and do puzzles and study in here. Miss Star teaches an English class, too. Would you like to join us?

Ivan: Oh yes, thank you. I want to learn better English.

Sam: Come on outside. You have to see this.

Narrator 2: Sam, Ivan, and Maria go into the backyard.

Maria: This is our playground. Miss Addams and her friends made it for us. It's the very first public playground in Chicago. That means we don't even have to pay to play out here.

Ivan: Look at the swings! And there's a place to play ball! I want to stay out here all day!

Narrator 1: Jane Addams walks into the yard.

Jane: Oh, good, you're out in the fresh air. That's very important. However, it's time for your sculpture class. You children should have the chance to be creative and make beautiful things. You can come back here and play later. Let's go, now!

Narrator 2: They all walk over to the art room, where Jane leaves the children. They sit down and pick up lumps of soft clay.

Ivan: What is this? What do I do with it?

Sam: It's clay. You can shape it and make things.

Ivan: I will make a flower for my mother. She loves flowers. We had a small garden at home in Russia, but she does not have time to grow flowers now.

Maria: Good idea! I'll make a flower for your mother, too.

Sam: Me, too. We'll make a whole garden for her!

Narrator 1: Albert and Jane walk into the sculpture class.

Albert: How do you like working with clay, Ivan? Do you have any questions?

Ivan: Yes, I do like this. The clay looks like nothing at first, but now look at my flower. Hull House has many good things, I think. What else can I do here?

Jane: You can be in the play with the other children. It's called *The Trolls' Holiday*. People who live here wrote the words and the music.

Sam: The members of the music school are going to sing. Our drama teacher shows us how to act. We are learning to tumble like trolls in the gym.

Narrator 2: A few hours later, Mrs. Lubov comes back. Albert brings the baby. Ivan comes in, carrying the clay flowers.

Albert: Here's Anna. She had a nap and ate dinner. She didn't cry at all!

Mrs. Lubov: Thank you. If my baby is happy, then I am happy. This is a good place for children.

Jane: This is a good place for you, too. We have English classes for adults. You can visit with other women.

Ivan: *(hands Mrs. Lubov the flowers)* Look what I made for you! Hull House is wonderful, Mama! Miss Addams and the others are kind and helpful. I am so happy that we came to Chicago in America!

Mrs. Lubov: Yes, Jane Addams is a good woman. My friends tell me that she is rich and could live in a beautiful house somewhere else in the city, but she lives like we do. She spends her money to help us. She gets others to help, too. Miss Addams, my children and I are so lucky to be here.

Jane: We are glad you found us, Mrs. Lubov. Keep coming to the classes and the women's meetings. Soon you will be helping the newcomers yourself.

Narrator 1: Jane Addams kept working to help poor people in Chicago. She worked for world peace and women's rights, too. In 1931 she received the Nobel Peace Prize. She lived at Hull House until she died on May 21, 1935.

Design a Playground

Jane Addams built the first public playground in Chicago. What would you put in a playground? Draw your playground here. Then finish the sentences about your playground.

My playground has _____

_____

_____

At my playground, children can _____

_____

_____

Name _____

Helping Others

1. Jane Addams worked hard. She helped many people, especially women and children. She helped solve many problems by offering child care, classes, places to play, and many other things. How can you help people or help solve problems in your neighborhood? Write your ideas on the chart.

Person or Problem	How I Can Help

2. Draw a picture. Show yourself helping someone else.

Name _____

Thank You, Jane Addams

Imagine that you are an immigrant child. Write a letter to Jane Addams. Thank her for the help she gave you and your family. Be sure to tell about the kind of help you got and how it helped you.

_____
Date

Dear Miss Addams,

_____

_____

_____

_____

_____

_____

_____

_____

_____

_____

_____

_____

Sincerely,

_____

Now Presenting...

Davy Crockett: Fact or Legend?

Davy Crockett was a frontiersman, hunter, soldier, businessman, and a lawmaker. His actual deeds, as well as legends about him, have made him an American hero.

Setting the Stage

Background

David "Davy" Crockett lived from 1786 to 1836. He had several careers including businessman, hunter, state legislator, and congressman from Kentucky. Crockett enjoyed telling stories about his adventures and often exaggerated for effect. His tales brought him wide recognition. During his lifetime, a play and several books about him became popular. These were loosely based on Crockett's real accomplishments, and it became hard to separate the facts from the legends. After his death at the Battle of the Alamo, the legends continued to grow.

Staging

You may choose to have readers set up in front of the board. Draw a large television set on the board behind them. Write the title of the play at the top of the "television screen."

Encore

Davy Crockett's autobiography is called *The Narrative of the Life of David Crockett of the State of Tennessee.* It can be accessed online (http://etext.lib.virginia.edu/railton/projects/price/crockett.htm). You may wish to use this site to show students how to use original source documents. Read passages aloud, and then have students discuss and summarize the information.

Students can also use the Internet to find more legends about Davy Crockett. Encourage them to each write a short summary of one legend, and then compile the summaries into a class book.

Vocabulary

Introduce and discuss the following words before reading the script. Encourage students to give examples of a "fact" and a "legend." Have them identify the words that relate to government.

Congress: the law-making part of the U.S. government, made up of the House of Representatives and the Senate

descendant: a person who is the son or daughter of a particular relative or ancestor

escape: to break free or get away

fact: a thing that has actually happened

legend: a story that is handed down for generations and is believed to have been based on actual events

legislature: a group of people who are given the power and responsibility to make laws for a nation

swamp: a piece of wet land that is always or often covered with water

Now Presenting...

Davy Crockett: Fact or Legend?

Contestants on a game show identify information about American hero Davy Crockett as either fact or legend.

Characters

D. V. Crockett............................ _____

Wanda Know (emcee) .... _____

Player #1 .... _____

Player #2 .... _____

Factito Chorus........................... _____

_____

_____

Legendaire Chorus .... _____

_____

_____

Announcer................................. _____

Davy Crockett: Fact or Legend?

.... **Characters** ....

D. V. Crockett
Wanda Know
Player #1
Player #2

Factito Chorus
Legendaire Chorus
Announcer

Announcer: Welcome to *Famous Person: Fact or Legend?* Our famous person for today's show is Davy Crockett. Born in Tennessee in 1786, Davy Crockett is the subject of many tall tales and legends. Many of his real-life adventures were just as amazing as the legends told about him. Today our two contestants will try to figure out which events from his life are facts, and which are legends. And now here's our hostess, Ms. Wanda Know.

Wanda Know: Hello, everyone. It's great to be here! And now let's meet our experts. They will make the final judgment about our contestants' answers. First, meet the Factitos.

Factito Chorus: *(chanting)* It's a fact; it's a fact.
We know it to be true—
it's something we can prove.

Wanda Know: The Factitos look for facts in encyclopedias and other books, and also on Internet sources. And now please welcome our other panel of experts—the Legendaires.

Legendaire Chorus: *(chanting)* It's a legend; it's a story.
It may be partly true,
but we don't know for sure.

Wanda Know: The Legendaires like stories. They don't worry about the truth. They don't check sources either.

Announcer: We also have a special guest with us today. Mr. D. V. Crockett, a descendant of Davy Crockett, is here with us. He will tell us the true story behind the legends. Now let's get started!

Wanda Know: Contestants, are you ready? Here is the first piece of information. Davy Crockett had a pet parrot. He tried to teach the bird to say his name but the bird could only say "Davy." That's how he got his nickname.

Player #1: That sounds true to me. I don't think parrots are too smart, even if they can speak.

Player #2: I never heard about him having a parrot. I think it's a legend.

Legendaire Chorus: *(chanting)* It's a legend; it's a story.
It may be partly true,
but we don't know for sure.

Announcer: There you have it! Our experts have ruled that Player #2 is correct—that information is a legend! Let's give Player #2 the first point. And now, perhaps Mr. D. V. Crockett can tell us the true story behind the legend.

D. V. Crockett: You bet! Actually, my ancestor used the name "David." A writer gave him the nickname "Davy." After that, other writers used the name "Davy" when they told stories about him.

Wanda Know: All right then—on to our next piece of information. When he was 12, David walked seven miles in two hours in deep snow. He was escaping from a man who wanted to keep him on his ranch.

Player #1: That must be a legend. I know I could never do anything like that!

Player #2: Kids back then did all kinds of things that we don't do now. And Davy Crockett was an extraordinary guy. I bet it's true.

Factito Chorus: *(chanting)* It's a fact; it's a fact. We know it to be true— it's something we can prove.

D. V. Crockett: You're right again, Player #2. We know that it's a fact because David wrote about it in his autobiography. David had worked helping a man drive a herd of cattle across Virginia. The man liked his work so much that he wanted to force Davy to stay on and keep working for him. But, as the story says, Davy would not let even deep snow or a seven-mile walk stop him from seeking his freedom!

Announcer: Well, Player #2 is in the lead with two points. Come on, Player #1. Let's see if you can take this one!

Wanda Know: In 1814 David was the best alligator wrestler in the swamps of Florida. He could wrestle a dozen alligators at a time.

Player #1: No way! That must be a legend!

Player #2: Hmm, he fought bears and was a good hunter. I think it could be true.

Legendaire Chorus: *(chanting)* It's a legend; it's a story.
It may be partly true,
but we don't know for sure.

Announcer: Mr. Crockett, what was the real story?

D. V. Crockett: David was in Florida, but he was in the army. He was fighting the British and the Indians who were helping them. He tracked them through the swamps.

Announcer: And Player #1 is now on the board with one correct answer! Let's have our next question.

Wanda Know: David Crockett was a member of the Kentucky legislature. A few years later he became a congressman.

Player #1: No, I don't think this could possibly be true. Davy Crockett could hardly read or write. There's no way he could have been a lawmaker.

Player #2: I'm going to have to disagree. I think I read about this somewhere. I'm going to go ahead and say this one is true.

Factito Chorus: *(chanting)* It's a fact; it's a fact.
We know it to be true—
it's something we can prove.

Announcer: So that's another correct response for Player #2?

D. V. Crockett: That's right. Player #1 is correct in saying that David did not read or write well. But Player #2 is also correct— David served the people of Kentucky as a lawmaker. He really knew how to listen to people. That's what made people think he would truly represent their interests. In fact, David served in the state legislature and later as a congressman.

Announcer: Now here's our last question.

Wanda Know: We know that David fought at the Battle of the Alamo in Texas in 1836. However, some say that he escaped in a hot-air balloon. Then he lived on an island for the rest of his life.

Players #1 and #2: We're not sure, but we hope it's true.

Legendaire Chorus: *(chanting)* It's a legend; it's a story.
It may be partly true,
but we don't know for sure.

D. V. Crockett: David fought bravely, but he was killed in the Battle of the Alamo. However, his heroic deeds live on.

Announcer: Thank you both for playing. You will each get a book about David Crockett and an imitation coonskin cap. And Player #2 will join us again tomorrow as we look at the life of another legendary figure.

Wanda Know: For now, let's sign off with some words from David Crockett himself: "I'll leave this truth for others when I am dead—just be sure you are right and then go ahead."

Stretching the Truth

When someone **exaggerates**, they use some true information. Then they add funny or impossible actions to stretch the truth and make the story more entertaining. This is one way that a legend is created.

Here are some true statements about David Crockett. Use the information and exaggerate to change them into legends.

1. David Crockett was a good hunter.

_____

_____

2. David Crockett was strong.

_____

_____

3. David Crockett was a soldier.

_____

_____

4. David Crockett was a lawmaker.

_____

_____

Main Idea and Detail

A **main idea** is the most important thing about a story. The details tell more about the main idea. Reread the play "Davy Crockett: Fact or Legend?" Then circle the sentence below that tells the main idea. Write the details from the play that support the main idea.

Main Idea:

David Crockett was a good storyteller.

David Crockett is a famous American hero.

David Crockett lived a long time ago.

Details:

1. _____

   _____

   _____

2. _____

   _____

   _____

3. _____

   _____

   _____

4. _____

   _____

   _____

Now Presenting...

A Riddle-Maker Saves the Day
Based on a Folktale from Vietnam

In this version of a traditional Vietnamese folktale, a clever boy uses a riddle to outwit a greedy man.

Setting the Stage

Background

The folktales of many countries include stories about clever children who outwit adults. This play is based on such a tale from Vietnam, called "The Fly."

Staging

Draw and cut out a housefly from paper. Have one student hold up the fly at appropriate times during the reading of the play.

Encore

This play is adapted from a Vietnamese folktale called "The Fly." Read this and other multicultural tales with students in *Favorite Folktales from Around the World,* edited by Jane Yolen.

After reading the play, have students work in teams to brainstorm lists of other living things that the man and boy could have used as a witness.

Vocabulary

Introduce and discuss the following words before reading the script. Then have partners use each word in a sentence.

bargain: an agreement in which two people settle on what each shall give or do

debt: something owed by one person to another

magistrate: an official with the power to make legal decisions

peasant: a person who works the land

wealthy: having many things or much money

witness: a person who saw something firsthand and can tell about it

Synonym Search

A **synonym** is a word that means about the same thing as another word. Look at each row of words. The first word is a word from the play. Two of the three words next to it are synonyms. Circle the two words that are synonyms for the first word.

Words from the Play	Choose Two Synonyms		
1. clever	(smart)	(quick-witted)	silly
2. enormous	old	large	huge
3. tiny	small	fancy	miniature
4. items	thoughts	things	objects
5. depart	leave	sleep	go
6. select	choose	pick	hug
7. wealthy	handsome	rich	prosperous
8. precious	valuable	shiny	important

Now choose one word from the chart. Write the word below.

Draw a picture to show the meaning of the word and its synonyms.

_____

Readers' Theater, Grade 3 • EMC 3308

Name _____

What Happened in the Play?

Use the words in the box to fill in the blanks.

bargain	debt	man's head
riddle	witness	rock

1. The wealthy man wanted the peasant to pay his _____.

2. The man wanted to know the answer to the boy's _____.

3. The man and boy made a _____.

4. The man and boy said the housefly could be a _____.

5. The boy told the magistrate the housefly was on the _____.

6. The man said the housefly was on the _____.

What happened at the end of the story? Draw a picture here.

Now Presenting...

The Walking Sticks Buy Shoes

The Walking Stick children all need new shoes. Mr. and Mrs. Walking Stick show them how to budget their own money to buy what they need.

Setting the Stage

Background

Make sure that students know that a walking stick is a long, thin insect that resembles a leaf or twig. It can grow up to 12 inches long. Its six legs are spaced far apart, with three on each side of its thorax. The walking stick spends most of its time hiding on twigs or leaves. It is a vegetarian and is nocturnal. There are about 3,000 varieties of walking sticks in the world. Most live in tropical and semitropical regions, but a few live in Canada and parts of the United States. Walking sticks can be successfully kept in terrariums as pets.

Vocabulary

Introduce and discuss the following words before reading the script:

budget: a fixed amount of money available for spending

benefit: the positive aspects of something you buy

consumers: people who buy and use things

opportunity cost: the main thing you have to give up in order to buy something else

After reading the script, encourage partners to use each of the words in sentences.

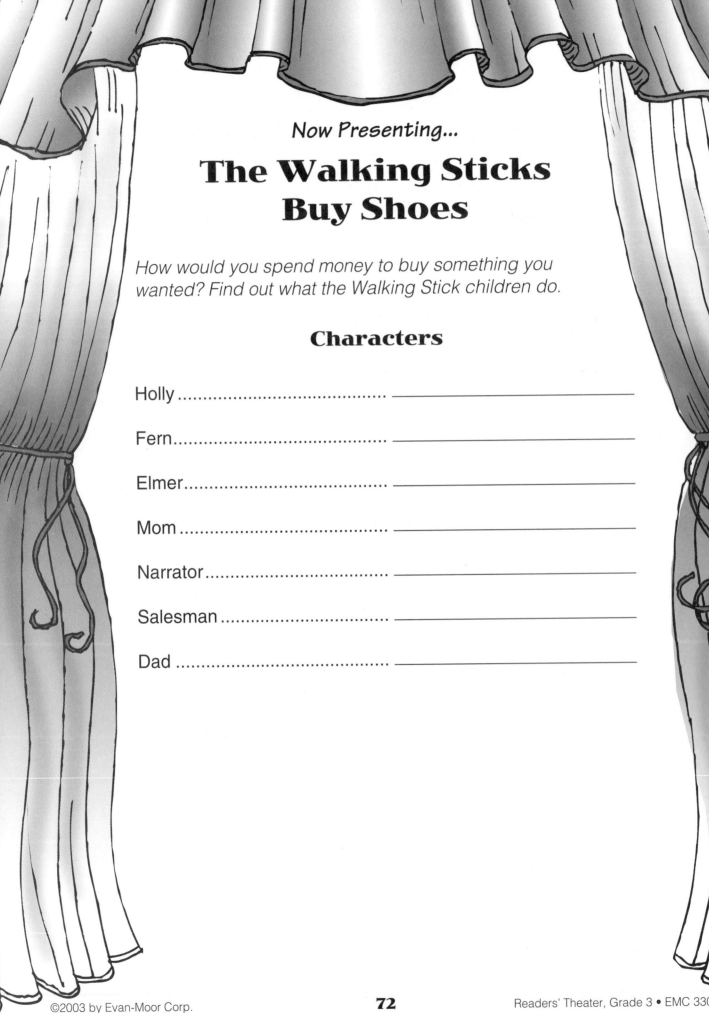

Now Presenting...

The Walking Sticks Buy Shoes

How would you spend money to buy something you wanted? Find out what the Walking Stick children do.

Characters

Holly .... ————————————————

Fern..................................... ————————————————

Elmer................................... ————————————————

Mom .... ————————————————

Narrator............................... ————————————————

Salesman .... ————————————————

Dad .... ————————————————

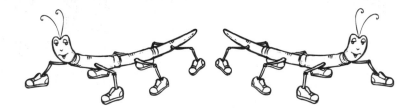

The Walking Sticks Buy Shoes

···················· Characters ····················

Holly   Narrator
Fern   Salesman
Elmer   Dad
Mom

Narrator: Our story takes place in a rainforest. The Walking Stick family is resting on a few of their favorite leaves late one evening.

Holly: Mom, all six of my sandals are too small. I need new ones.

Fern: Two of my sneakers have holes in them. And I don't even like them anymore. They're so out of style!

Elmer: I need new shoes for the track team. Tryouts are next week.

Mom: It's time for a trip to Rainforest Footwear. We'll all go on Saturday night. I'll tell your father.

Narrator: During the week Mr. and Mrs. Walking Stick talk about ways to help their children learn about spending money. At daybreak on Saturday morning, they explain their plan.

Dad: Your mother and I want you to be responsible consumers who use money wisely. Instead of us paying for whatever you want this time, you'll each get a budget.

Holly: What's that?

Mom: A budget is a limited amount of money that you have to spend. Your dad and I will give each of you $75. You may spend your money any way you want, but that is all you will get. Think about what you want before we get to the store.

Fern: If we want shoes that cost more than our $75, can we spend our own money?

Dad: Yes, that's fine with us.

Elmer: Can we keep the extra if we don't spend it all?

Mom: Yes, you may. Now, why don't you look at the newspaper ads, think about what you want, and get a good day's sleep. Be ready to go at sunset.

Narrator: The kids go to bed. That evening they take the Perky Parrot Express to the Canopy Mall and go directly to Rainforest Footwear.

Salesman: Good evening, may I help you?

Holly: Wow, look at all the cool shoes. Yes, please, I'd like to try one pair of red, one pair of orange, and one pair of yellow sandals.

Salesman: Right away, miss. Have a seat here.

Fern: I like these Purple Puddle Jumpers, but they cost $25 a pair. If I buy three pairs, that's my whole $75. I want to buy new antenna glitter, too.

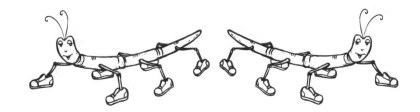

Dad: Think about the benefit you'll be getting. Remember, that's the positive value that these shoes have for you. Of course, you also need to think about the opportunity cost—or what you'll have to give up in order to get the thing that you really want or need.

Fern: So if I buy the Purple Puddle Jumpers, the glitter is my opportunity cost. I'll have to give up buying the glitter if I spend all my money on the shoes. The benefit, though, would be having really cool, in-style shoes. Hmm, I have to think about this one.

Elmer: Dad, look at these Super Lightfoot Twig Trackers. They are awesome. I'd get my fastest times ever in them! But they cost $40 a pair. If I get three pairs, I'd have to use my own $45, too. I was planning to buy the new Mighty Mosquito video game.

Fern: *(grabbing one of his arms)* You, dear brother, need to think about your benefits and opportunity cost. Come over here, and I'll explain it all.

Holly: *(walking up with three shoeboxes)* I'm finished. The sandals are on sale for $12.99 a pair. That came to $38.97. My change is $36.03. My budget is in great shape! Now I want to look around the rest of the mall. Mom, will you come with me?

Dad: Go ahead, Magnolia. I'll stay here with these two. We'll meet you at the Lovely Leaf Café in half an hour.
(to Elmer and Fern) Have you two decided yet?

Fern: I have. I'll replace my two worn out sneakers with these $20 ones now. Then I'll buy the Purple Puddle Jumpers on sale next month. I'll sit for Mrs. Spider's kids to earn extra money. I can have the shoes and the glitter, too. I won't have an opportunity cost.

Dad: What a wise decision. How about you, Elmer?

Elmer: I gotta have these Twig Trackers. They feel great, and I know they'll help my speed. *(taking a big gulp)* The video game is my opportunity cost. I'll get the Twig Trackers and work hard on the track team.

Dad: It sounds like you really thought about it, Elmer. I'll charge the shoes and you can pay me back when we get home.

Elmer: Thanks, Dad.

Narrator: They pay for the shoes.

Salesman: Good-bye now, and thanks for your business.

Narrator: The family has lunch at the Lovely Leaf Café.

Mom: How did you like using a budget?

Holly: It was easier to buy stuff when you and Dad paid for it, but I liked feeling responsible for my money.

Fern: I liked it, too.

Elmer: All that decision-making made me hungry. Let's eat! *(They all laugh as they eat their leaves).*

Name _____

Budget Planner

Pretend you are a walking stick. You have $75.00 to spend on shoes. Remember, you need three pairs for your six feet! Use the budget planner to keep track of what you spend.

Budget Planner

Plain Sneakers ....$15.75   Leaf Lander Boots ... $19.00

Firefly Light-Ups .....$25.00   Twin Trackers.......... $50.00

Summery Sandals...$10.99   Water Walkers........ $21.50
on sale

Shoes	Cost	Budget Balance
Example: Leaf Lander Boots	$19.00	$75.00 – $19.00 = $56.00
Pair 1:		
Pair 2:		
Pair 3:		
Total Cost:		
Money Remaining:		

Did you have an opportunity cost? _____

What was it? _____

Design Walking Stick Shoes

What would walking stick shoes look like? Draw shoes on this walking stick. Then write a name for each shoe under it.

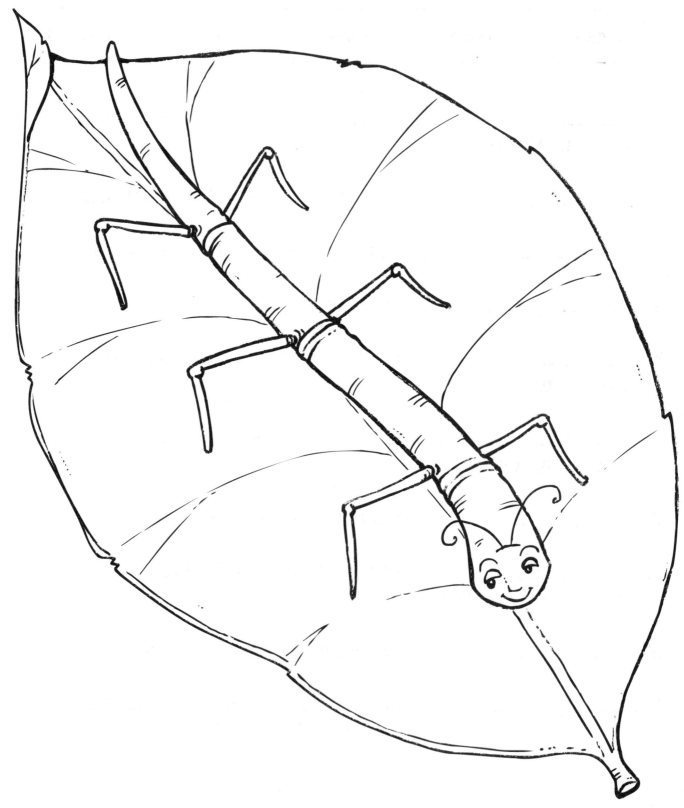

Name _____

Which Walking Stick?

Use the words in the word box to finish the sentences.

Holly	Fern	Elmer	Mom	Dad

1. _____ did not want to wear sneakers that were out of style.

2. _____ wanted new shoes for the track team.

3. _____ explained the budget to the children.

4. _____ wanted sandals.

5. _____ told the children about benefits and opportunity costs.

6. _____ gave up the video game as the opportunity cost.

7. _____ had extra money left over.

8. _____ waited until the Purple Puddle Jumpers went on sale.

9. _____ said Fern made a wise decision.

10. _____ was hungry after making decisions.

Now Presenting...

It's the Pits!

The La Brea Tar Pits in Los Angeles, California, contain thousands of fossils from the Ice Age. The George C. Page Museum of La Brea Discoveries exhibits the fossils, and they continue to be studied there.

Setting the Stage

Background

The La Brea Tar Pits were formed over two million years ago when oil leaked through cracks in the earth's surface. Bones belonging to mammoths, mastodons, saber-toothed cats, bison, wolves, birds, and insects have been found in the layers of asphalt. The fossils were first studied around 1906 by scientists from the University of California at Berkeley. Research at the pits is ongoing. *La Brea* (lah BREH-ah) means "the tar" in Spanish. (Spanish speakers find it amusing that the site is called "The 'The Tar' Tar Pits"!)

Before reading the script, encourage students to brainstorm what they already know and what they want to find out about fossils. Use the KWL chart from the activity on page 86. After reading the script, students will complete the chart, filling in information they learn.

Staging

Encourage the person reading the Bubble Voice part to sound like a computer voice.

Encore

Students can take a virtual trip to the La Brea Tar Pits by visiting the Web site (www.tarpits.org).

Help students create their own fossil dig. Pour a thin layer of dirt or sand in a dishpan. Next, put in small items such as toothpicks, toy animals, and bottle caps. Cover this with more dirt. Allow students to dig for "fossils" and describe what they find.

Vocabulary

Introduce and discuss the following words before reading the script:

layers: multiple thicknesses of a substance, stacked one on top of the next

mammoth: an extinct elephant with long curved tusks and hairy skin

pool: a small pond

saber-toothed cat: an extinct cat, similar to a tiger, with long curved upper-canine teeth

Now Presenting...

It's the Pits!

How did fossils form in the tar pits? Two children find out.

Characters

Narrator 1 .... _____

Narrator 2 .... _____

Chorus .... _____

Marty .... _____

Sally .... _____

Bubble Voice .... _____

It's the Pits!

········· Characters ·········

Narrator 1	Marty
Narrator 2	Sally
Chorus	Bubble Voice

Narrator 1: Would you expect to see fossils in the middle of a big city? You can if you visit the La Brea Tar Pits. They are right in downtown Los Angeles, California.

Narrator 2: Join Marty and Sally as they take an unusual tour of the tar pits. As our story begins, they are walking along a path, looking at the open tar pits.

Marty: Wow, this is so cool! The fossils in the museum next door came from these tar pits.

Sally: Look at this statue of a mammoth trapped in the tar. Don't you wonder how animals like that got stuck?

Marty: I sure do. I wonder what this place was like thousands of years ago, too. I wish there was a way to find out.

Narrator 1: Suddenly, a large clear plastic bubble appears in front of them. They see two seats inside the bubble. A voice from the bubble speaks to them.

Bubble Voice: Come in. Sit here and your questions will be answered.

Marty: I wonder what that means?

Sally: Let's go in and find out.

Narrator 2: They sit down and a whirring noise starts. The bubble spins around and around. Then it stops.

Marty: What happened? Where are we?

Bubble Voice: You are still at the La Brea Tar Pits, but you're in the Ice Age, about 40,000 years ago.

Sally: Wow, it's a lot cooler and wetter—and really smelly. It smells like a street being paved. I see lots of big plants, but no buildings. This doesn't look anything like the Los Angeles I know.

Marty: Look at the pools of bubbling tar! They're all around us. Some of them look like they're almost covered over with leaves and dust. They're kind of hard to see. *(pointing)* And that pool of tar even has some water on top of it. You can't really tell that there is tar under it.

Sally: Look! Here comes a mammoth. It looks just like the statue. It's headed right for the pit that's covered with water! I bet it's going to try to take a drink.

Chorus, Sally, and Marty: Watch out for the pits—oh no— or it's into the tar you will go. It's gooey and it's icky, and it's very, very sticky. You will turn into a fossil if you go right into the tar pits—oh no!

Marty: It's too late! The mammoth's feet are getting stuck. It looks like it's getting more stuck every time it moves.

Sally: Yipes, those saber-toothed cats are running toward the mammoth. It looks like they're planning on having a mammoth meal. And look—the mammoth is going farther into the tar pit as it tries to get away from the cats.

Marty: Now they're all stuck. I guess this is the way the animals got trapped. Wow, what a sight!

Sally: *(to the Bubble)* How did the animals turn into fossils?

Bubble Voice: Hold on and I'll show you.

Narrator 1: The whirring noise starts again. The bubble spins around and around. Then it stops.

Marty: We're still at the tar pits, but I don't see the mammoth or the saber-toothed cats.

Bubble Voice: We have moved 20,000 years closer to our time. What do you think happened to the beasts?

Sally: I think that their bodies decayed. Then their bones sank deeper into the pit.

Bubble Voice: That's right. Then in the winter the tar got hard. The bones were preserved in the tar. In the warmer months, more tar bubbled up and covered over the top with a new layer.

Sally: And now I see some other animals stuck in the pit.

Chorus, Sally, and Marty: Watch out for the pits—oh no—
or it's into the tar you will go.
It's gooey and it's icky,
and it's very, very sticky.
You will turn into a fossil if you go
right into the tar pits—oh no!

Marty: I bet they will decay and their bones will be in another layer in the pits, right?

Bubble Voice: Correct. This process happened year after year. Over thousands of years, wolves, lions, horses, birds, and even insects got stuck in the tar. In a way, each tar pit looks like a giant cake with many layers. The oldest fossils are on the bottom layer, and the youngest are at the top.

Marty: It's lucky for us that the animals got stuck. Now scientists have thousands of fossils to study.

Sally: When did they start to study the fossils here? Can you show us that on the way back to the present?

Narrator 2: The whirring noise starts again. The bubble spins around and around. Then it stops.

Marty: This looks more like our time, but there aren't as many pits, and the museum and statues are not here.

Bubble Voice: You are looking at one of the first fossil digs. The year is about 1906.

Sally: Look at those men—they're throwing away the small bones. They shouldn't do that.

Bubble Voice: A wise observation. In those days, the scientists only kept the largest bones. Now they know better and send all of the bones to the lab. But your journey time is up now. Prepare to return to the present.

Narrator 1: The whirring noise starts again. The bubble spins around and around. All of a sudden it stops. The children are back in the present and the bubble is gone.

Marty: Hey, do you think that trip really happened?

Sally: I'm not really sure.

Marty: Sally, look at your shoe! It's covered with black tar!

Chorus, Sally, and Marty: Watch out for the pits—oh no—
or it's into the tar you will go.
It's gooey and it's icky,
and it's very, very sticky.
You will turn into a fossil if you go
right into the tar pits—oh no!

A KWL Chart

In the first column, write things you know about fossils. In the middle column, write things you want to find out. After you read "It's the Pits!", use the last column to write the things you learned.

What I Know	What I Want to Find Out	What I Learned

Name _____

Make a Tar Pits Book

Copy the sentence from the box that goes with each picture. Then color and cut out the pictures, put them in order, and staple them together. If you do more research about the La Brea Tar Pits, add pages to the book.

The bones sank into the tar.	**Scientists clean and study the fossils.**
Animals walked or ran into the tar pits.	**Scientists take the fossils out of the tar.**

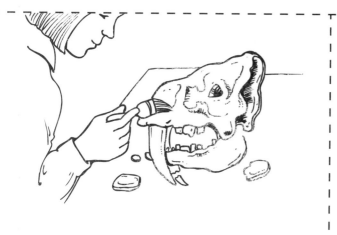

_____

_____

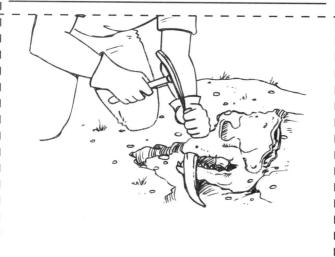

_____

_____

Name _____

True or False?

Read the sentences. Next to each one, write **true** or **false**. Then rewrite the false sentences to make them true.

1. The La Brea Tar Pits are about 100 years old.   _____

_____

_____

2. The sticky tar trapped animals, birds, and insects.   _____

_____

_____

3. The bones stayed on the top of the tar pits.   _____

_____

_____

4. The tar got cold in the summer.   _____

_____

_____

5. Scientists study the fossil bones.   _____

_____

_____

Now Presenting...

Yankee Doodle Hits the Road

Join Yankee Doodle as he travels through the newly formed United States with George Washington, who is headed to New York City for his inauguration.

12 parts

Setting the Stage

Background

In 1781 the Americans won the Revolutionary War against the British. The leaders of the United States of America immediately set to work to build the new nation. In 1787 the Constitution of the United States was written at the Constitutional Convention, under the leadership of George Washington. The Constitution created the presidency. In 1789 Washington was unanimously elected to become the first president of the new nation. He rode from his home in Mount Vernon to the capital in New York City, where his inauguration took place. All along the way he was greeted with parades and other festivities.

Use a map of the East Coast to show Washington's route to his inauguration. Point out these places and make sure students can pronounce them: Alexandria, Virginia; Baltimore, Maryland; Delaware; Trenton, New Jersey; Philadelphia; and New York.

The tune "Yankee Doodle" was written by the British during the French and Indian War to make fun of the colonial army. The colonists adopted the song and wrote additional verses. The verses in this script are new variations created in this historic tradition.

Staging

The person reading Yankee Doodle's part may use a paper towel tube or something similar to represent a microphone.

Encore

You may wish to read an actual account of Washington's journey to the inauguration online (www.publicbookshelf. com/public_html/Our_country_vol2/georgewas_bfb.html).

To learn more about the life and times of our nation's first president, students may check out *George Washington: A Picture Book Biography* by James Cross Giblin, or *America in the Time of George Washington* by Sally Isaacs.

Vocabulary

Introduce and discuss the following words before reading the script:

arch: a curved structure, used as a monument or gateway

barge: a large, flat-bottomed boat used on a river

capital: the city where the government of a country or state is located

inauguration: the ceremony of installing a person in office

nation: country

pilot: a person who steers a ship or boat

president: the highest officer or leader of a country

triumphal: victorious or successful; in celebration of someone or an event

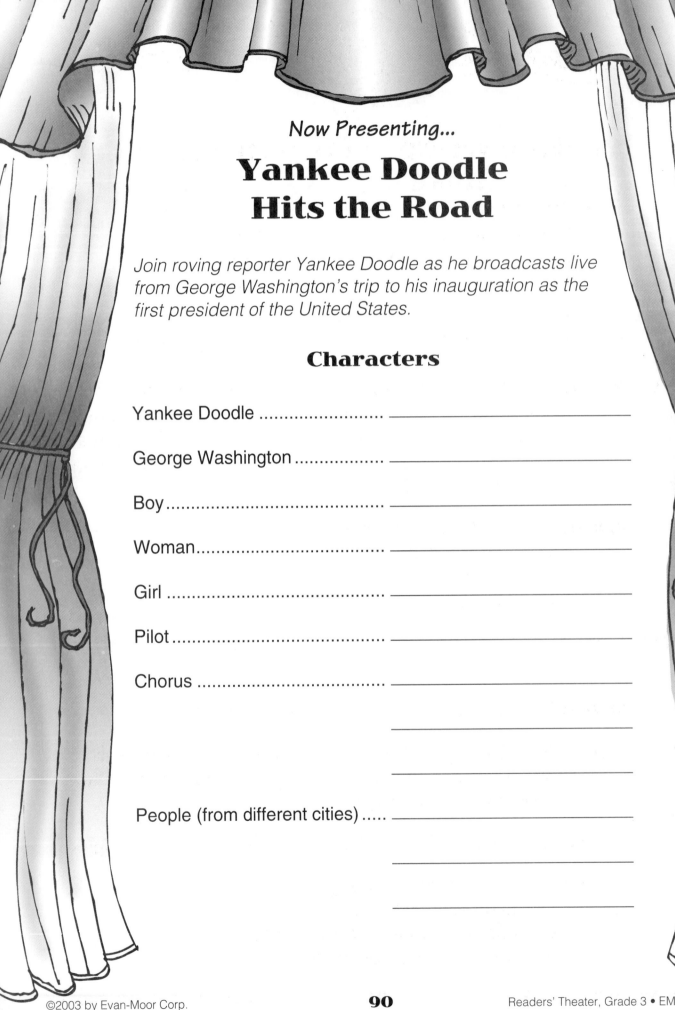

Now Presenting...

Yankee Doodle Hits the Road

Join roving reporter Yankee Doodle as he broadcasts live from George Washington's trip to his inauguration as the first president of the United States.

Characters

Yankee Doodle .... _____

George Washington .... _____

Boy .... _____

Woman....................................... _____

Girl .... _____

Pilot .... _____

Chorus .... _____

_____

_____

People (from different cities) ..... _____

_____

_____

Yankee Doodle Hits the Road

······················· **Characters** ·······················

Yankee Doodle   Girl
George Washington   Pilot
Boy   Chorus
Woman   People

Yankee Doodle: Good morning. It's April 6, 1789. I am at Mount Vernon, Virginia, the home of George Washington. On April 30, he will become the first president of the United States of America. Join us as we travel to our nation's capital, New York City, for this event.

Chorus: Yankee Doodle, on we go
to this great celebration.
Let's hear it for George Washington
and for our brand new nation.

Yankee Doodle: Our first stop is Alexandria, Virginia. Let's join the public dinner, now in progress.

People: Long live the king, George Washington!

Washington: No, I will not be a king. I will not wear a crown. This country is like no other before it. The people will rule. I will be their president.

People: No kings for America! Long live President Washington!

Chorus: Yankee Doodle, on we go
to this great celebration.
Let's hear it for George Washington
and for our brand new nation.

(a few days later, at a feast in Baltimore)

Yankee Doodle: Listen to the church bells! Let's hear from the people of Baltimore.

People: George Washington was a brave soldier and a great commander of the army. He will be the best leader for our country.

Washington: I'm proud of you! Maryland is our seventh state. Baltimore is growing. You have a large, busy harbor.

Yankee Doodle: *(talking with his mouth full)* These crabs are yummy. I'll be back on the air soon. Mmm, mmm.

Chorus: Yankee Doodle, on we go
to this great celebration.
Let's hear it for George Washington
and for our brand new nation.

(several days later, in Philadelphia)

Yankee Doodle: Hello from Philly. The people of the City of Brotherly Love have built a 20-foot tall triumphal arch. It's covered with flowers and green branches. Let's hear from Mr. Washington and the crowd.

Washington: I am honored. The arch is beautiful, and the flowers smell lovely.

People: Long live George Washington, the father of his country!

Boy: *(handing a flag to George)* Sir, here is a new American flag for you. Betsy Ross showed us how to make them. Everyone wants one.

Washington: *(waving the flag)* Thank you. Please tell Mrs. Ross I said, "Hey."

Yankee Doodle: That's it from Philadelphia. Join us next time as we report in from our next stopping point in Trenton, New Jersey.

Chorus: Yankee Doodle, on we go
to this great celebration.
Let's hear it for George Washington
and for our brand new nation.

(another day, in Trenton)

Woman: We made an arch over this bridge. The 13 pillars on the arch stand for the original 13 colonies.

Girl: We made a banner that says "The Defender of the Mothers will be the Protector of the Daughters." George Washington is our hero.

Washington: Thank you. I'm proud to serve my country. Your sons, brothers, and husbands were brave soldiers. I wish I could stay longer, but I must move on.

Yankee Doodle: We are outside of Trenton now, at Elizabethtown Point, on a large barge in the river. There are 13 pilots dressed in sparkling white uniforms.

Pilot: *(to Washington)* Sir, on behalf of all the pilots, it is an honor to transport you. Wait until you see New York harbor. It's decorated with flags. Boats of well-wishers are waiting for us.

Chorus: Yankee Doodle, on we go
to this great celebration.
Let's hear it for George Washington
and for our brand new nation.

Yankee Doodle: We're landing. People are lined up on the shore cheering and shouting. A band is playing!

People: Long live liberty! Three cheers for the red, white, and blue!

Yankee Doodle: That's it for today. Join me tomorrow as George Washington becomes the first president of the United States.

(the next day on the outside balcony of Federal Hall, in New York City)

Yankee Doodle: Hundreds of people have gathered here outside Federal Hall. Here comes Mr. Washington now, and does he ever look dapper! He's wearing a dark brown cloth suit and white silk stockings. I'm told his entire outfit was made in America. His hair is powdered white and pulled back with a ribbon. Let's hear some of his speech.

Washington: This is indeed a great occasion. I thank all of you for your trust in me, and I will work hard to deserve it. We must preserve our liberty. Our new form of government is an experiment and it will take the cooperation of the American people to make it a success.

People: We will do it! Liberty and justice for all Americans! Long live President George Washington!

Yankee Doodle: Tune in again this evening for the fireworks and celebration. Until then, this is Yankee Doodle, signing off.

Chorus: Yankee Doodle, on we go
to this great celebration.
Let's hear it for George Washington
and for our brand new nation.

Travel with George Washington
and Yankee Doodle

George Washington traveled through many cities and states when he became the first president.

Draw a line to show the route George Washington took and number the stops he made.

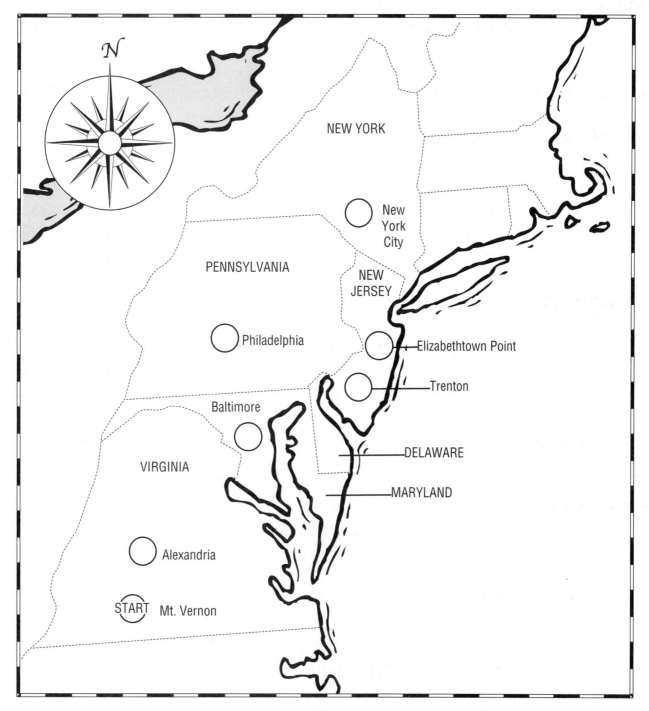

Name _____

Honor George Washington

People decorated their cities to honor George Washington. Some built arches and others made banners. Design your own way to honor George Washington, the first president of the United States.

Celebration Match

Many cities held celebrations for George Washington. Match each city with the type of celebration it had.

_____   1. Alexandria   a. barge with 13 pilots

_____   2. Baltimore   b. arch and banner

_____   3. Philadelphia   c. public dinner

_____   4. Trenton   d. triumphal arch

_____   5. Elizabethtown Point   e. feast

_____   6. New York City harbor   f. flags and boats

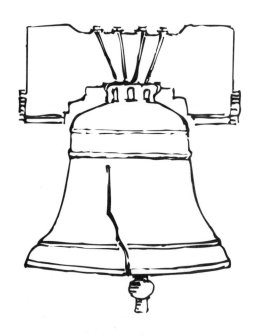

Now Presenting...

Brer Rabbit Shares His Crops

Brer Rabbit rents farmland from Brer Bear, but Brer Bear insists on sharing the crop as payment. Brer Rabbit finds an unusual solution to his problem.

Setting the Stage

Background

Tales of tricksters like Brer Rabbit appear in many cultures. They usually involve a cunning character who gets the better of a richer or more powerful character. In 1881 Joel Chandler Harris published his first collection of Brer Rabbit tales, narrated by a fictional character named Uncle Remus. These stories had been collected among African American slaves in the South. The tales, passed along in the oral tradition, included elements from African folktales. The word *brer* is an abbreviated form of "brother," a word which is used in other versions of these stories.

Staging

Have students make and wear construction paper ears to represent Brer Bear and Brer Rabbit. They may also draw pictures of potato, oat, and corn plants.

Vocabulary

Introduce and discuss the following words before reading the script. Then have students identify the words that relate to farming.

acres: a unit for measuring land; one acre is 43,560 square feet

collect: to gather up

crop: plants grown and gathered by people for their use

rent: a payment made for the use of property

Help students use context to identify the two meanings of the words *share* and *plant* as they are used in the story.

Name _____

Sharing the Crops

Brer Rabbit and Brer Bear are sharing their crops. How much does each farmer get? Draw pictures and write the answer to the problem.

1. Brer Bear shares 18 cabbages. How many does each farmer get? 18 ÷ 2 = _____ 	2. Brer Rabbit shares 30 ears of corn. How many does each farmer get? 30 ÷ _____ = _____ 
3. Brer Bear shares 48 strawberries. How many does each farmer get? _____ ÷ _____ = _____ 	4. Brer Rabbit shares 50 potatoes. How many does each farmer get? _____ ÷ _____ = _____

Name _____

Brer Rabbit Shares His Crops

Find and circle the words in the word search. The words go across and up and down. Then use the words to complete the sentences.

Z	V	D	N	M	G	C	J	P	S
F	C	E	F	F	A	R	M	L	H
N	E	I	G	H	B	O	R	A	A
R	E	N	T	S	U	P	L	N	R
P	R	O	A	C	R	E	B	T	E
I	C	P	E	V	M	F	L	Z	C
A	C	O	L	L	E	C	T	G	G

plant
acre
farm
neighbor
crop
share
rent
collect

1. A place to grow crops and raise animals is a _____.

2. Someone who lives near you is your _____.

3. When you pay money to someone to use their land, you _____ it.

4. An _____ is a piece of land that is almost the size of a football field.

5. A _____ is a plant that is grown for food.

6. When you _____ something, you ask for payment.

7. When you _____ something, you put a seed in the ground so it can grow.

8. When you _____ something, you give some of it to someone else.

Now Presenting...

Space Camp Is a Blast!

Space Camp is a five-day program for adults and children from ages 9 to 18. Campers receive basic astronaut training; accommodations are made for campers with visual and hearing impairments.

Setting the Stage

Background

At Space Camp, the campers work in teams. They learn what it's like to live and work on a shuttle. They use some of the same simulators as the astronauts use in their training, and they work in Mission Control. Counselors help the campers build and launch model rockets, and discuss the history of the space program. At the end of the week, the teams take turns operating the shuttle and working at Mission Control to simulate a real launch.

Staging

You may choose to have students make mission patches similar to those worn by the astronauts. Then they pin or tape their patches on the top of their left sleeves.

Encore

For more information about Space Camp, visit the official Web site (www.spacecamp.com), or check out some of these books to learn more about the space program: *To Space and Back* by Sally Ride and Susan Okie, *The Eyewitness Book of Space Exploration* by Carole Stott, and *Aboard the Space Shuttle* by Florence Steinberg.

Vocabulary

Introduce and discuss the following words before reading the script:

astronaut: a person trained to participate in a space flight

Braille: a system of printing and writing designed by Louis Braille for use by visually impaired people; it consists of patterns of raised dots

Five Degrees of Freedom Chair (5DF): a piece of astronaut-training machinery that permits movement in five directions

gravity: a force that pulls all objects in Earth's atmosphere toward the center of Earth

Extra-Vehicular Activity (EVA): a spacewalk

Manned Maneuvering Unit (MMU): a small power source used to facilitate mobility in a gravity-free environment

Mission Control Center: the base of communications between a spacecraft and scientists on Earth

Multi-Axis Trainer (MAT): a piece of astronaut-training machinery that allows you to spin freely, as if in a gravity-free environment

simulator: a training device that artificially duplicates the conditions likely to be experienced under other circumstances

space shuttle: a spacecraft designed to take people and equipment into space on a mission and then return to Earth

weightless: free from the effects of gravity

Now Presenting...

Space Camp Is a Blast!

Where can you go to use the same equipment that the astronauts use, build rockets, and do science experiments? Go to Space Camp and have a blast!

Characters

Narrator.. _____

Marla .... _____
(a visually-impaired girl)

Tran... _____
(a hearing-impaired boy)

Carlos.. _____

Katie.. _____

Mr. Astro .... _____
(a Space Camp counselor; he interprets for Tran)

Ms. Starr .... _____
(a Space Camp counselor; she helps Marla)

Space Camp Is a Blast!

.... Characters ....

Narrator   Katie
Marla   Mr. Astro
Tran   Ms. Starr
Carlos

Narrator: These children are spending five days at Space Camp, working as a team. On the first two days, they did science experiments and launched model rockets. We join them on their third day of camp as they start astronaut training.

Mr. Astro: These simulators will let you experience the same things that astronauts experience in their training.

Tran: Can we use the Multi-Axis Trainer? I want to spin around and around.

Mr. Astro: Yes, we can do that right now. Tran, you can go first. I'll attach the harness and put the straps on your hands and feet.

Tran: Wow! I'm spinning in all different directions! It starts out so fast, and then it slows down. So this is what it feels like when the spacecraft comes back to Earth!

Narrator: The campers take turns using the MAT. Next they try the Five Degrees of Freedom Chair, or 5DF.

Ms. Starr: The 5DF looks like a chair at the end of a long pole. The chair moves in five directions. It trains you to do an EVA. Does anyone remember what that is?

Katie: That's an Extra-Vehicular Activity, or a spacewalk.

Mr. Astro: Have a seat, Carlos. I'll put the harness and helmet on you, and then I'll go operate the controls.

Carlos: This chair floats on air! I'm going backward—oh, now forward. Now the chair is moving from side to side. Yikes! It's rolling me around. It's going down! And now straight up. You guys have to try this!

Narrator: The campers all try the 5DF. Then they use the Manned Maneuvering Unit, or MMU.

Carlos: If we were astronauts in space, this MMU would be like a big jet backpack on our spacesuits instead of this chairlike thing, right?

Ms. Starr: Yes, that's right. Since we have gravity on Earth, we need to use this machine to imitate the feeling of weightlessness in space. Who remembers why the astronauts need to use the MMU?

Tran: It lets them move outside the shuttle or space station to do an EVA. That's an Extra-Vehicular Activity, or a spacewalk. Hey, look at Marla!

Marla: Oh, I like this feeling. It's slow, but I can move in every direction. I can imagine being outside the space station, helping to add on another section. This is great!

Ms. Starr: Line up for your turn, kids. Then we'll try an underwater escape!

(later the same day, at the lake)

Carlos: I read about this. It's called "the dunker." It looks like the crew capsule section of a shuttle. We will sit inside, and it will be lowered into the water.

Tran: So we'll practice getting out of the escape hatch underwater, just like the astronauts might have to do if their spacecraft lands in the water. Mr. Astro and I can use sign language underwater.

Mr. Astro: Knowing sign language will be a real advantage for us, Tran!

Ms. Starr: Marla, you'll be attached to me with this cord. Just tug on it if you need anything.

Marla: I like that idea!

Narrator: The campers each practice escaping from the dunker. Everyone makes it out without any trouble. Then they spend some more time in the water, learning how to steer and paddle a life raft. They spend the rest of the day watching videos about living and working in space.

(the next day, at Mission Control Center)

Mr. Astro: This is where the space shuttle flight is directed. From here, you can watch the launch and flight and talk to the shuttle crew.

Marla: How can I work the controls and use the computers?

Katie: Feel this, Marla. All of the controls and the computer keyboard have Braille on them.

Ms. Starr: And the computers will speak to you. You can talk to them to give commands. The computer screen is also set up to use large print. And the manuals are all printed in large type, too.

Mr. Astro: Now each of you take a seat in front of a control unit. Tran, you can use e-mail to talk to the others. There are also cameras set up all around the room. If you sign into the camera, you will be shown on the monitors.

Tran: Thanks, Mr. Astro.

Katie: This is so cool! I feel like I'm working at a real shuttle launch.

Carlos: I'm glad we can spend the whole day here. I want to learn how the spacecraft are operated.

(later, after dinner)

Mr. Astro: Tomorrow we'll put together everything you learned all week. You will take turns in the shuttle and at Mission Control. We'll simulate a real launch.

Katie: Then I'm going to bed now, so I'll be ready in the morning.

Ms. Starr: You know what? That's just what the astronauts do the night before a launch. They know how important it is to be well rested.

Tran: Well, I sure want to have the complete astronaut experience! I'm going to bed.

Marla and Carlos: Me, too. Good night!

Name _____

Acronyms

An **acronym** is a word that is formed by using the first letter or syllable from the words in a title. Sometimes the first two letters—or a letter in the middle of the word—are also used. An acronym can be spelled out or pronounced as a word. Acronyms are always written in all capital letters.

Here are a few familiar acronyms:

CD
compact **d**isk

ZIP
Zone **I**mprovement **P**lan

RV
recreational **v**ehicle

The military and the space program use many acronyms. Match the acronyms below with the correct titles. Then underline the letters that are used to make the acronym.

_____ 1. NASA   a. Self-Contained Underwater Breathing Apparatus

_____ 2. RADAR   b. Sound Navigation Ranging

_____ 3. SCUBA   c. Multi-Axis Trainer

_____ 4. MMU   d. National Air and Space Administration

_____ 5. EVA   e. Headquarters

_____ 6. MAT   f. Extra-Vehicular Activity

_____ 7. SONAR   g. Manned Maneuvering Unit

_____ 8. HQ   h. Radio Detecting and Ranging

Make your own acronym!
Write a title or a phrase that you use a lot below. Then write the acronym.

_____   _____

Name _____

Fill It Out!

An **application** is a form that you fill out when you sign up for something, such as a camp or any other program. The application asks for information about you. It also asks you to explain the reasons you want to participate in the activity. Complete this application for Space Camp.

Space Camp Application

Name _____ Age _____

Answer the following questions.

1. Why do you want to go to Space Camp?

_____

_____

2. At Space Camp, you have to work with a team. Why do you think this is important?

_____

_____

3. What will you do now to get ready to come to Space Camp?

_____

_____

The Braille Alphabet

People with vision impairments use the Braille alphabet to read. Hold this page in one hand. Use a pin to poke a hole in each of the black dots. Do this from the <u>back</u> of the page. Then feel the bumps. This is similar to what Braille letters feel like.

A	B	C	D	E	F	G	H	I
J	K	L	M	N	O	P	Q	R
S	T	U	V	W	X	Y	Z	

of	the	with	and	for

In the box below, use the pin to "write" one word in Braille. Then ask a friend to "read" your word with his or her fingers.

Now Presenting...

Putting It Together

Four soccer teammates make sand sundaes as a fundraiser for their team. They run into problems working individually, but when they switch to assembly line production, their business takes off.

6 parts

Setting the Stage

Background

Explain the principle of the assembly line by telling students that in 1913, Henry Ford developed a moving assembly line to manufacture his automobiles. Each worker on the line was responsible for completing the same task over and over again, building the same small portion of each car. While this was somewhat monotonous for the workers, the division of labor allowed Ford to produce better automobiles more quickly and at a lower price.

Encore

After students brainstorm products for the activity on page 123, encourage them to think about how their product might be produced on an assembly line. You may even wish to try "manufacturing" some of the products proposed by students.

Vocabulary

Introduce and discuss the following economic-related words before reading the script. You might like to distribute pages from the financial section of the newspaper to partners and have them skim their pages, highlighting any of the financial vocabulary words that they find.

business: the buying and selling of goods and services, usually for a profit

cost: the amount spent in producing or making a product

investment: money that is put into a business with the purpose of making a profit

loss: money lost in operating a business

manufacturer: a person or company in the business of manufacturing a product

profit: money made from a business transaction

Putting It Together

Members of a soccer team want to raise money to buy bleachers for their soccer field. How can they do it? Can a lesson from modern industry help them?

Characters

Narrator .... _____

Mike .... _____

Bobby .... _____

Linda .... _____

Dee .... _____

Tina (Dee's sister) .... _____

Putting It Together

···················· **Characters** ····················

Narrator	Linda
Mike	Dee
Bobby	Tina

Narrator: Mike, Bobby, Linda, and Dee are talking on their way home from soccer practice.

Mike: Did you hear the bad news? The town council has to spend their extra money fixing the potholes on Main Street. Now we won't be getting those new bleachers that we need at the soccer field.

Dee: That means the fans will have to bring their own chairs again this year.

Linda: There must be something we can do.

Bobby: There must be a way that we can raise that money. If the city government can't buy the bleachers, we'll just have to do it ourselves!

Dee: I agree. Let's talk it over when we get to my house. I'm sure we can come up with something.

Narrator: Soon the teammates are discussing several ideas in Dee's kitchen. Her older sister, Tina, is busy at the kitchen counter, spooning colored sand into a plastic ice-cream sundae dish.

Tina: Hey, kiddos, what's up?

Narrator: The friends tell Tina their problem.

Tina: *(still spooning sand into the dish)* That's too bad. I'm sure you'll be able to think of something.

Dee: What are you doing, anyway?

Tina: I'm making a sand sundae.

Mike: That sounds awful? Who would want to eat that?

Tina: No—it's not something to eat! You put a photograph on the inside of the dish, fill the jar with sand, and then pour melted wax on the top. It looks like an ice-cream sundae, but it's actually a cool way to display a photo. I thought it would make a great birthday gift for Mom.

Linda: Cute! Now that's an idea that could make money!

Bobby: I bet people would buy them if we put in pictures of their kids or pets.

Mike: What a great idea! We can use all the school pictures we've been collecting from our friends. We know plenty of people who would want to buy them.

Linda: We can use our savings to buy the supplies. That will be our investment.

Tina: The craft store sells all of the supplies you need. It costs about $1.00 to make one sundae.

Bobby: If we sell them for $3.00 each, we'll make back our investment and a good profit, too.

Tina: Go for it, guys! Why don't you meet back here next Saturday and tell me how it's going?

Teammates: Okay, it's a deal.

(the next Saturday, at Dee's house)

Mike: *(frowning)* This wasn't as easy as I thought. Look at these disasters! First, I couldn't get the pictures to stay straight. Then I spilled wax down the side of the glass and it hardened on the outside before I could clean it off. After I messed these up, I didn't even try to make any more. It was bye-bye investment for me.

Bobby: *(sighing)* I made six, but I haven't had the nerve to ask people to buy them. This is a loss for me, too!

Linda: *(looking upset)* My little sister dumped my sand into her sandbox. I couldn't afford to buy more sand, so I lost the money I invested in the supplies.

Dee: Well, I sold five so far, and I actually made a profit! But it was hard work! My mom helped me with the hot wax, but she said she can't spend as much time setting up and doing this project with me anymore.

Tina: Are you kids open to a suggestion?

Linda: Sure.

Tina: Have you ever heard of Henry Ford?

Bobby: Sure! Didn't he start the Ford car company?

Tina: That's right. He used an assembly line to make the cars. Each worker did one part of the job, and then the car moved on to the next worker. By organizing workers on an assembly line, he was able to make cars faster and for less money than other manufacturers.

Dee: So maybe we could use an assembly line to make the sand sundaes. We'd each do one of the jobs, and we'd make them a lot faster.

Mike: I bet they'd look better, too, because we'll each become really good at the job we're doing.

Tina: Why don't you work in our garage? If you like, I can help you get set up. If you make enough sundaes, you can sell them next month at the craft bazaar.

Bobby: Let's go for it!

Narrator: The kids bring all of their supplies to Dee and Tina's garage. They arrange everything on a long table and sit down next to each other.

Linda: First, I'll pour the sand halfway up the dishes and make pretty patterns. I'm good at that.

Dee: Then I'll put the pictures in nice and straight, and add the rest of the sand.

Bobby: I'll pour the wax after Tina melts it.

Mike: And I'll pack the finished sundaes in these boxes.

Narrator: The friends finish 100 sand sundaes in time for the bazaar. They sell all of them, then meet at Dee's house after the bazaar to add up their profits.

Mike: We collected $300.00.

Linda: Our expenses were $100.00.

Bobby: That means we made $200.00 profit! We make a great team—in soccer AND in business!

Dee: Way to go! We've made a great start on the bleacher money. Let's go give Coach this money now!

Mike: And then let's get back here and make some more sand sundaes!

Name _____

Sell It!

To sell something, you have to convince people to buy it. Think of a product you could sell to earn money for something special. Use this space to make an ad for your product. Then write down three reasons why someone should buy your product.

_____

_____

_____

_____

123

Name _____

Business Math

To figure out your **profit**, you subtract the cost of making your product from the total sales amount collected.

Example:
$300.00 total sales
− $100.00 cost to make
$200.00 profit

How much profit will you make on each of these sales?

$900.00 total sales
− $450.00 cost to make

$57.50 total sales
− $35.00 cost to make

$123.00 total sales
− $16.95 cost to make

$4,510.00 total sales
− $1,037.00 cost to make

When you make a **profit**, you have more money than when you started. When you have a **loss**, you have less money. Make an **X** in the column for a profit or a loss.

Starting Amount	Ending Amount	Profit	Loss
$776.95	$2,395.05		
$987.00	$284.65		
$83.22	$46.32		
$6,457.88	$9,412.11		

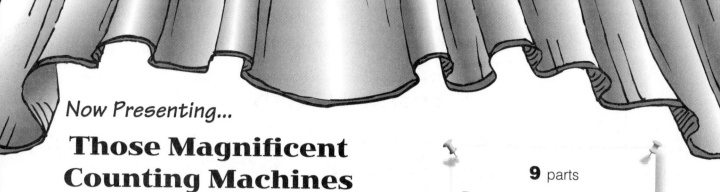

Now Presenting...

Those Magnificent Counting Machines

Although personal computers have been in use for only about 30 years, the history of the calculating machines that led to the development of the modern computer goes back much farther.

Setting the Stage

Background

For centuries people have built machines to help them count and solve complicated mathematical problems. These machines were the forebearers of the modern computer. The abacus and Pascal's numerical wheel calculator were early computing devices. Leonardo da Vinci sketched a mechanical calculator that has since been built. As technology progressed, computers became more sophisticated, but were still mostly used by universities and the military. Businesses began using them in the 1960s. The development of the personal computer in 1976 caused a revolution in the industry. Now there are over 100 million computers worldwide.

Staging

Have the students reading Luis and Hanh's parts wear sunglasses and hats to resemble the virtual reality apparatus. Encourage the students reading the computer parts to use voices that sound like computer-generated voices.

Encore

Have students interview people of different age groups to learn about their experiences with computers. Invite students to share their findings with the class.

To read more about the history of the computer, students can check out the following Web sites and books:

- The IEEE Computer Society Web site (www.computer.org/history/development)

- Computer Chronicles from Stone to Silicon (http://library.thinkquest.org/22522)

- *How Did We Find Out About Computers?* by Isaac Asimov

- *A True Book of Personal Computers* by Chanan and Tom Kazunas

Vocabulary

Introduce and discuss the following words before reading the script:

gear: a toothed wheel designed to mesh with another to help move machinery

keyboard: the rows of keys on a computer terminal

mechanical: operated by machinery or a mechanism

monitor: a video screen for displaying data

program: to plan a computer program to perform a specific function

virtual reality: computer-produced images that create the impression of experiencing a three-dimensional environment

Readers' Theater, Grade 3 • EMC 3308

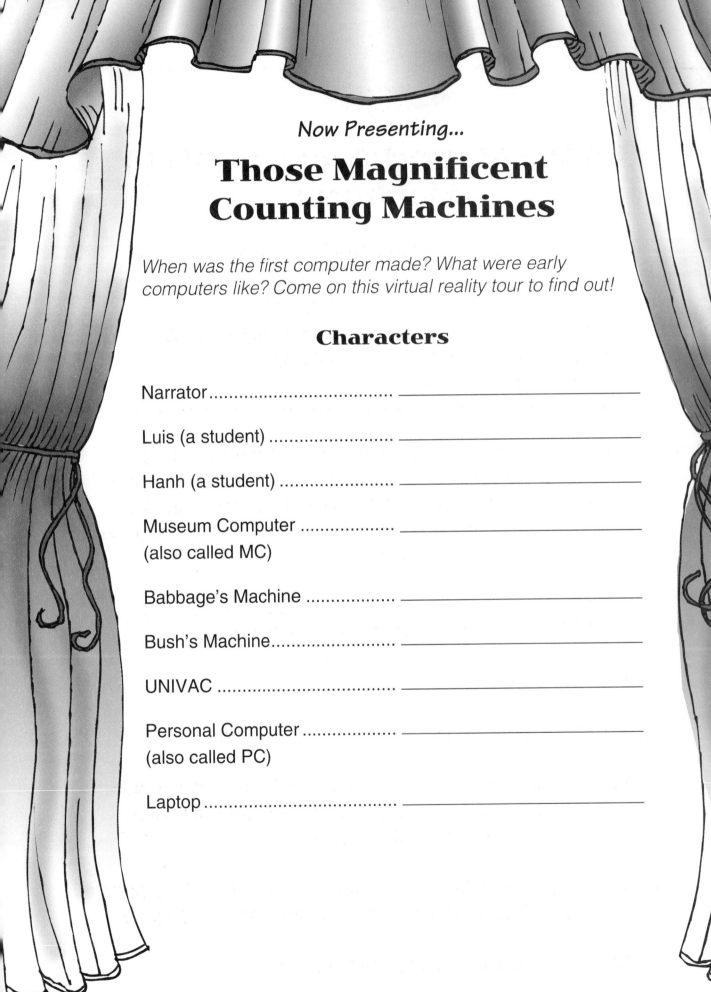

Now Presenting...

Those Magnificent Counting Machines

When was the first computer made? What were early computers like? Come on this virtual reality tour to find out!

Characters

Narrator..................................... _____

Luis (a student) .... _____

Hanh (a student) .... _____

Museum Computer .... _____
(also called MC)

Babbage's Machine .... _____

Bush's Machine........................ _____

UNIVAC .... _____

Personal Computer .... _____
(also called PC)

Laptop .... _____

Readers' Theater, Grade 3 • EMC 3308

Those Magnificent Counting Machines

.... **Characters** ....

Narrator

Luis

Hanh

Museum Computer

Babbage's Machine

Bush's Machine

UNIVAC

Personal Computer

Laptop

Narrator: It's the year 2050. Luis and Hanh are researching the history of computers. They use a Sense-a-Vision Computer at their school. It links to a computer in a museum in another state. They get a virtual reality tour that uses all of their senses.

Hanh: Let's put on our headsets and goggles and link up. MC, please show us the very first computer.

MC: Accessing.

Luis: Hey, wait a minute. That's a human brain!

MC: Correct. A computer is any device that helps you add, subtract, multiply, and divide. Your brain does these things. So it is the first computer.

Hanh: Okay, but we know there were inventions to help people count. Please show us the first mechanical computer.

MC: I will take you to Babbage's machine.

Babbage's Machine: Mr. Babbage made me in England in 1833. I looked like a tall clock, and used wheels and gears. He had bright ideas, but he didn't have all of the right tools or parts, so I was never finished. However, he is known as the Father of the Computer because he was the first to use the basic parts of a modern computer.

Luis: Wow! Those gears sure are noisy!

Hanh: Look! Someone has to be there all the time to move the gears. What a pain! What developed after this?

MC: Many other calculating machines were made. In 1925 an American named Mr. Bush made a different kind of machine.

Luis: It takes up a whole room! It's hot and noisy. What are those glass bulbs?

Bush's Machine: They are vacuum tubes. They help run my electric motors. I was the first modern computer because I had motors. I could store information and be programmed.

Hanh: But where's the monitor? Where's the keyboard?

Bush's Machine: There weren't any. People moved switches, wires, and rods. The information was printed out on paper.

Luis: It's a shame Mr. Babbage didn't live to see you. MC, when were all-electronic computers built?

MC: In 1946 two Americans named Maunchly and Eckert made the first one. It was called ENIAC as a nickname. Then in 1951 they built a better model called UNIVAC.

Hanh: Look at that! UNIVAC fills a whole room, too. Whew, it's hot in here! There are so many people running around flipping switches and changing burned out vacuum tubes.

UNIVAC: People thought that the whole world would only need about 12 computers like me.

Luis: Wow, were they wrong! We have a computer for each of the kids in our school. Everyone has at least one computer at home, too.

UNIVAC: *(sighing loudly)* I felt so powerful, but even your wrist computer is much more powerful than I was.

Hanh: When did computers get smaller and better?

MC: In 1948 three scientists made a small device called a transistor. It didn't burn out like the vacuum tubes. This let computers get smaller and faster. Some of them only took up one wall in a room. But computers were still used mostly in labs.

Luis: Look at this display, Hanh. It's about the 1970s. It shows computers in banks and other companies. I can hear the whirring and humming of the motors. It feels warm in this room, but not as hot as the UNIVAC room. No one is changing tubes, either.

Hanh: They're so much smaller. This one fits on the top of an office desk. But there's still no monitor or keyboard. When did computers get those?

MC: In 1976 Steve Jobs and Steve Wozniak made the Apple II. It had a keyboard and a monitor. It was one of the first personal computers, or PCs.

PC: By the 1980s, computers used little parts called "chips." These made us even faster and more powerful. We were smaller, too. I was about the size of a small television set. I fit on a desk. Machines like me were in many homes and schools.

Luis: And video games became popular, right?

PC: That's right. In 1981 about two million people owned PCs. By 1991 there were over 65 million PCs in homes all over the world. And lots of them were used to play video games!

MC: Let me show you the computers of the 1990s.

Hanh: The computers are smaller than some that we have seen, but each one still takes up the whole top of a school desk. And they still had to be plugged in to use electricity. Did those computers talk and follow voice commands like mine does?

MC: No, most machines had keyboards. Talking computers were just being developed. By about 2010, all computers could follow voice commands and talk to the users.

Luis: People's hands must have been sore and tired! They couldn't take the computer with them like we do, either. They all had to be plugged in for electricity.

MC: Let's look at the laptop computers of the late 1990s and early 2000s.

Laptop: Now I was really something different! I used batteries, so you could take me anywhere. I could fit on your lap or in a backpack. I weighed less than 10 pounds. Some computers were even smaller, about the size of a paperback book or the palm of your hand.

Hanh: That's more like what we have today.

MC: There is one very big difference. Until about 20 years ago, computers were used mostly to work math problems, type up text, and to find information. They did not run houses, drive your car, operate on sick people, or fly planes by themselves.

Luis: But one thing has not changed. Computers then only did what the people told them to do. It's still that way now.

MC: Yes, and it will probably stay that way. I hope you got the information you need. You may disconnect now.

Hanh and Luis: Thanks, MC. See you later!

Name _____

Computers of the Future

What do you think a computer might look like in the year 2050? How will it work? What will it do? Draw your picture here. Then write five sentences about your computer.

1. _____

2. _____

3. _____

4. _____

5. _____

 Readers' Theater, Grade 3 • EMC 3308

The History of Computers

Write the type of computer used during each time period. Draw a picture of what you think each computer might have looked like. Then cut out the two sections and glue them together to form a time line.

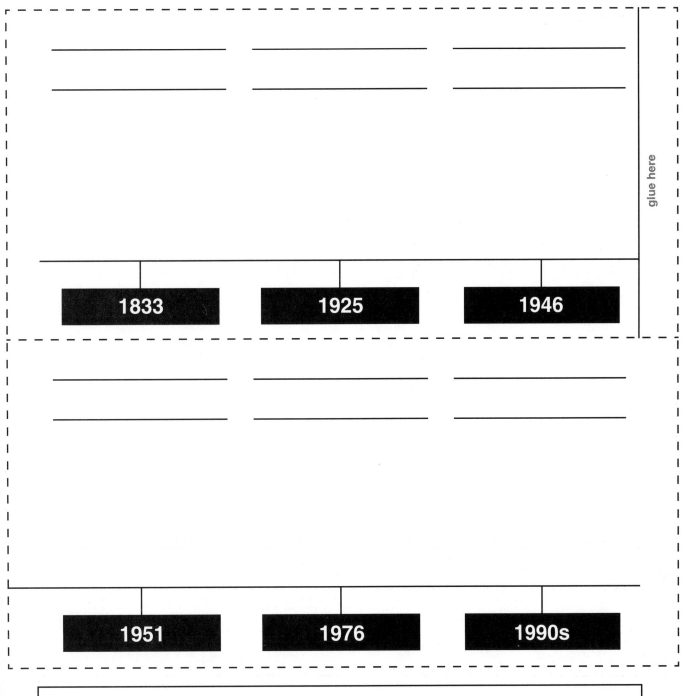

glue here

| 1833 | 1925 | 1946 |

| 1951 | 1976 | 1990s |

| laptop | PC | UNIVAC |
| Bush's machine | Babbage's machine | ENIAC |

Now Presenting...

Space-Wrecked!

Tourists on their way home from a vacation are suddenly stranded on an uninhabited planet. Their ingenuity helps them survive.

Setting the Stage

Background

Remind students that science fiction combines elements of science with those of fiction. The science may be current and realistic, or it may be a projection of what may be developed in the future. The present, past, and future—here or on other worlds—can be used as the setting.

Staging

Encourage students to use their imaginations to draw these characters from an unknown part of the universe, from some point in the future. They may display their pictures as they read their characters' lines.

Encore

After reading this script, students may enjoy reading fictional accounts of shipwrecks, such as *Robinson Crusoe* or *The Swiss Family Robinson.*

Vocabulary

Introduce and discuss the following words before reading the script:

architect: a person whose job is to design and draw plans for buildings and other structures

artist: a person who works in any of the fine arts, such as drawing, painting, sculpting, etc.

atmosphere: oxygen and other gases surrounding a planet

chemist: a specialist in dealing with the composition, properties, and reactions of substances

computer programmer: a person who develops programs for computers

distress: a condition of danger or trouble

engineer: a person specialized in operating engines or technical equipment

nutritionist: a person specialized in the sort of foods needed by the body for good health

paramedic: a person trained to provide emergency medical care

pilot: a person trained to operate the controls of a spacecraft

survive: to continue to live after some sort of disaster

Name _____

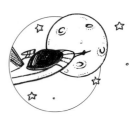

Creating a Community

Make an **X** in the column that tells what you think you must have, what you would like to have, and what you feel you don't need in a community.

	Must Have	Would Like to Have	Don't Need
Police and Fire Departments			
Shopping Malls			
Museums			
Food/Farms			
Parks			
Plumbing			
Swimming Pool			
Schools			
Entertainment			
Library			

Pick one of the items from the chart. Explain why you marked the column that you chose.

_____

_____

_____

_____

_____

_____

What's Next?

What do you think Ona's idea was at the end of the play? Write about it here.

_____

_____

_____

_____

_____

_____

_____

_____

Answer Key

Spider Woman and the Gift of the Loom
page 14: Drawings will vary.
page 15: Answers will vary.
page 16: 1. Raise the sheep.; 2. Sheer the sheep.; 3. Wash the wool.; 4. Straighten the wool.; 5. Spin the wool.; 6. Dye the wool.; 7. Set up the loom.; 8. Weave the rug.; 9. Remove the rug from the loom.

A Wild Day
page 23: **Birds and Butterflies:** heron, pelican, swallowtail; **Reptiles and Amphibians:** alligator, crocodile, tree frog; **Mammals:** manatee, raccoon, bobcat
page 24: 1. can't; 2. They're; 3. Let's; 4. That's; 5. I'll; 6. I'm; 7. We're; 8. You're; 9. isn't; 10. It's
page 25: Drawings will vary.

B. W. Hawkins and the Dinosaur Models
page 32: Artwork will vary. Check to see that models are assembled correctly.
page 33: Answers will vary.
page 34: 5. They made an iron skeleton.; 2. They made a small clay model.; 6. They made a brick base.; 3. They made a life-size clay model.; 1. They made a drawing.; 7. They covered the skeleton with cement.; 4. They made a mold for the body.

The Amazing Laundry Hamper
page 41: **Chuck:** friendly, helpful, neat, obedient; **Doris:** disobedient, greedy, lazy, messy
page 42: Answers will vary. Check to make sure that students use two adjectives per noun.
page 43: 1. Chuck obeyed his parents and Mrs. Dazzle. He did his work carefully and cheerfully. 2. Chuck got many silver dollars. 3. Doris was lazy and disobedient. She was not careful with her work. 4. Doris got mud stuck to her clothes. 5. People who do their work well will be rewarded with good things.

It Happened at Hull House
page 50: Answers will vary.
page 51: Answers will vary.
page 52: Answers will vary.

Davy Crockett: Fact or Legend?
page 60: Answers will vary. Check to make sure that students understand how to use exaggeration to embellish a true statement.
page 61: **Main Idea:** David Crockett is a famous American hero. **Details:** 1. He served in the army and fought the British and Indians.; 2. He was a member of the Kentucky legislature.; 3. He was a congressman from Kentucky.; 4. He gave his life at the Battle of the Alamo.

A Riddle-Maker Saves the Day
page 68: Answers will vary.
page 69: 1. smart, quick-witted; 2. large, huge; 3. small, miniature; 4. things, objects; 5. leave, go; 6. choose, pick; 7. rich, prosperous; 8. valuable, important. Drawings will vary.
page 70: 1. debt; 2. riddle; 3. bargain; 4. witness; 5. man's head; 6. rock; 7. Students should draw a picture of the man leaving empty-handed, or of the peasants cheering.

The Walking Sticks Buy Shoes
page 77: Answers will vary. Check to make sure that students have entered the cost of three pairs of shoes, and then subtracted the cost of each pair from $75.00.
page 78: Artwork will vary.

page 79: 1. Fern; 2. Elmer; 3. Mom; 4. Holly; 5. Dad; 6. Elmer; 7. Holly; 8. Fern; 9. Dad; 10. Elmer

It's the Pits!
page 86: Answers will vary.
page 87: Picture 1: Animals walked or ran into the tar pits.; Picture 2: The bones sank into the tar.; Picture 3: Scientists take the fossils out of the tar.; Picture 4: Scientists clean and study the fossils.
page 88: 1. false—The La Brea Tar Pits are over 2 million years old.; 2. true; 3. false—The bones sank to the bottom of the tar pits.; 4. false—The tar got hot in the summer. OR The tar got cold in the winter.; 5. true

Yankee Doodle Hits the Road
page 95: The line goes from Mount Vernon north to Alexandria–1, Baltimore–2, Philadelphia–3, Trenton–4, Elizabethtown Point–5, and New York City–6.
page 96: Students should draw a banner, arch, or other item and write a phrase honoring George Washington.
page 97: 1. c; 2. e; 3. d; 4. b; 5. a; 6. f

Brer Rabbit Shares His Crops
page 104: carrots–bottom; lettuce–top; corn–middle; beets–bottom; oats–top; celery–middle
page 105: 1. 9; 2. 15; 3. 24; 4. 25
page 106: 1. farm; 2. neighbor; 3. rent; 4. acre; 5. crop; 6. collect; 7. plant; 8. share

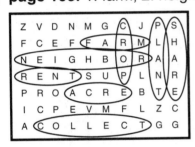

Space Camp Is a Blast!
page 113: 1. d–**N**ational **A**ir and **S**pace **A**dministration; 2. h–**Ra**dio **D**etecting **A**nd **R**anging; 3. a–**S**elf-**C**ontained **U**nderwater **B**reathing **A**pparatus; 4. g–**M**anned **M**aneuvering **U**nit; 5. f–**E**xtra-**V**ehicular **A**ctivity; 6. c–**M**ulti-**A**xis **T**rainer; 7. b–**So**und **Na**vigation **R**anging; 8. e–**H**ead**q**uarters
page 114: Answers will vary.
page 115: Answers will vary.

Putting It Together
page 123: Answers will vary.
page 124: $450.00; $22.50; $106.05; $3,473.00; profit; loss; loss; profit

Those Magnificent Counting Machines
page 132: Answers will vary.
page 133: 1833–Babbage's machine; 1925–Bush's machine; 1946–ENIAC; 1951–UNIVAC; 1976–PC; 1990s–laptop

Space-Wrecked!
page 141: Answers will vary.
page 142: Answers will vary.